gnomeland

Gnomeland

AN INTRODUCTION TO THE LITTLE PEOPLE

MARGARET EGLETON

Firefly Books

This book is for the gnomes—all of them

They make people smile

And people who like gnomes are happy people

A FIREFLY BOOK

Published by Firefly Books Ltd. 2008

First printing

Publisher Cataloging-in-Publication Data (U.S.)
Egleton, Margaret.
    Gnomeland : an introduction to the little people / Margaret Egleton.
[160]p. : col. photos. ; cm.
Includes index.
Summary: Collection of photographs and stories about the world of gnomes: from their
first mention in German folklore, to garden decorations, illustrations on post-cards, and
characters in film, song, and stories.
ISBN-13: 978-1-55407-406-8
ISBN-10: 1-55407-406-1
1. Gnomes. I. Title.
398.45 dc22   GR549.E   2008

Library and Archives Canada Cataloguing in Publication
Egleton, Margaret.
    Gnomeland : an introduction to the little people / Margaret Egleton.
Includes index.
ISBN 978-1-55407-406-8
ISBN-10: 1-55407-406-1
    1. Gnomes. I. Title.
GR549.E35 2008   .   398'.45   C2008-900368-3

Published in the United States by
Firefly Books (U.S.) Inc.
P.O. Box 1338, Ellicott Station
Buffalo, New York 14205

Published in Canada by
Firefly Books Ltd.
66 Leek Crescent
Richmond Hill, Ontario L4B 1H1

Developed by Kyle Cathie Ltd.
Printed in China by SNP LeeFung

contents

a world of gnomes

Home and garden styles change from generation to
generation, but one little iconic feature has remained
steadfast in our affections—the garden gnome. He is
changing and adapting to modern life but he refuses to go
away. There is no doubt that he is a worldwide
phenomenon and, despite what the cynics might say,
his popularity has not diminished.

folklore, myths and legends

Gnomes are legendary and gnome mythology is centuries old, involving woodland gnomes, dune gnomes, farm gnomes, garden gnomes, house gnomes and others, all of which have their own characteristics and names, depending on local tradition. Sometimes there is confusion about the different creatures in European folklore because mythical beings such as goblins and dwarfs are often represented as gnomes and vice versa. The confusion between gnomes and dwarfs is thought to be Anglo-American—gnomes, as spirits of the earth, have featured in English literature since the 16th century. Although having little to do with the modern garden gnome, in 1791, this spirit of the earth was among the spirits of the four elements depicted on the frontispiece of Erasmus Darwin's *The Botanic Garden*, in which he refers to gnomes as "the guards and guides of Nature's chemic toil."

Below left: **Max by the Philipp Griebel Company, from an original *c.* 1915 Bernhard Strobel & Co. mold.**

Below right: **Martin, another terra cotta gnome made by Philipp Griebel.**

Today, in Germany there are *zwergen*, in Sweden there are *tomten*, in Denmark, *nissen*, in Holland *kabouter*, and in France *nain*, while in the United States, there are gnomes—in modern parlance, they are all the same and can all be called gnomes.

Early representations in most traditions show gnomes as gnarled old men with long white beards or as misshapen dwarfs, mischievous sprites or goblins, and all characterized by their small size.

In Germany, gnomes are known as dwarfs (*zwergen*), but they also came to be thought of as being from the earth. They were often seen as miners or guardians of treasure buried deep underground. Swiss bankers were famously disparaged by British prime minister Harold Wilson as the "gnomes of Zurich." There is a theory that miners of small stature came from the island of Crete around 1500 BC to dig for gold and silver in parts of Europe, including southeast Germany, and they might have been the origin of the mining dwarf myth.

Left: Two 18th-century German garden statues of dwarfs (*zwergen*).

9

It is believed that the familiar pointed red hat that we see on many garden gnomes today was originally a representation of the hat that was once worn by the miners in the mountains of southeast Germany. The hat is thought to have been colored red so that it could be seen in the glimmer of lights in the mine, shaped so that it could be filled with padding to give protection from falling stones, and was extended to cover the neck and shoulders. It could be said that it was the forerunner of the modern safety helmet!

Dwarfs often featured in German fairy tales, such as those told by the Brothers Grimm, and dwarf figurines are thought to bring good fortune to a home if placed in the house or garden, which explains why they became so popular.

In Sweden, the mythological *tomte*, or gnome, is believed to be associated with the farm and its animals. He takes care of the farmer's home, his children and his animals and protects them from misfortune, particularly at night. He is seen as the bringer of gifts and became associated with Christmas. He is imagined as a small, elderly man with a full beard, dressed in the everyday clothing of a farmer. In 1880, when Viktor Rydberg's tale *Little Vigg's Adventures on Christmas Eve* was published, paintings by Jenny Nyström, who became known as the "mother of *tomten*," illustrated the book. She envisaged the mythical Swedish gnome as the red-capped, friendly figure with the white beard that has been associated with Christmas in Scandinavia ever since, and she established a lifelong relationship with

the character. When Rydberg later wrote his well-known poem "Tomten," Jenny provided the illustration and she went on to make a wide range of charming Christmas cards that have turned into the visualization of how Sweden's Christmas traditions were. So the kindhearted, Swedish, gift-giving *tomte* was born.

Away from the farm, the *tomte* was thought to live under the floorboards and give presents at Christmas. The *tomte* began to assume a role similar to the Santa Claus figures in other countries, and in Sweden it is a custom after Christmas Eve dinner for someone to dress up as the Christmas *Tomte* and distribute family presents.

The Danish word for a gnome is *nisse* and tradition has it that he is a little man, always dressed in gray, wearing a red hat and believed to be hundreds of years old. He can be heard at night as he walks around a farm watching over the animals and it is customary to leave food out for him to bring good luck. Toward the end of the 19th century, the North American Santa Claus figure began appearing in Denmark with the Christmas tree custom imported from Germany. He was then called *Julemanden,* meaning "Christmas man." Over the years Santa Claus became more and more connected with the *nisse,* who turned into the *Julenisse* or "Christmas gnome" and was then seen always with a red Santa Claus hat. For 11 months of the year however, the *nisse* is not normally seen in Denmark, but in December the country turns into *Nisseland.* Most

store windows are decorated with gnomes and
Danish houses have not one, but perhaps hundreds
of *nissen* on windowsills, furniture, shelves—just
about anywhere there is space for them. There is still
a tradition to put out a bowl of rice pudding for the
Julenisse on Christmas night, and tradition dictates
that it must have a good lump of butter and a sugar
and cinnamon topping. The *Julenisse* also enjoys a
glass of sweet beer. In January, the *nissen* are carefully
wrapped up and put away until next Christmas.

Opposite page top: A classic gnome hat, thought to have been
inspired by the German miners' red padded helmet.

Opposite page bottom: Santa gnome by Swedish artist Jenny
Nyström.

Right: A Christmas gnome by Philipp Griebel.

11

the first garden gnome

Today, except perhaps in Scandinavian countries, gnomes are generally thought of as a fun and whimsical garden accessory, but they were once much more highly regarded. The painted gnome we now know was created in Germany toward the end of the 19th century when there was a large ceramic industry making household and garden ornaments and manufacturers capitalized on the popularity of gnomes. Many of these early gnome figures were large and distinguished by the superbly sculpted detail of their faces and clothing, and were advertised as "garden figures." It is not surprising that they often found their way into affluent homes and gardens, some as garden statuary, but many as house ornaments and some as door guardians.

In April 1992, *The Garden* magazine, published by the Royal Horticultural Society (RHS) in the U.K., included an article by Brent Elliott, PhD, arguing that in 19th-century England, there was a prejudice against colored sculpture despite the uncomfortable revelation that even the ancient Greeks painted their statues. There was one area, however, in which colored sculpture had always been acceptable—porcelain—and by the 1890s English porcelain was being eagerly collected. In 1906, *The Connoisseur* magazine published an article describing the porcelain collection of a Lt. Col. Powney who had 22 "dwarfs." It was at that time that the first English advertisement for "garden" gnomes appeared when the German ceramics company Ernst Wahliss, which had galleries in London, offered what was claimed to be the largest collection of ceramic work in the city. They regularly placed a double-page ad in *The Connoisseur* and in 1908 offered "figures for the garden, animal figures and gnomes." The ad continued: "The gnomes and quaint manikins, which we stock in all styles and sizes, lend themselves particularly well for the artistic decoration of parks and gardens. One of our clients has over one hundred of these gnomes in his famous subterranean passages and gardens." The client was Sir Frank Crisp of Friar Park (see page 44). The Wahliss Galleries stated that they were "Sole proprietors of the original moulds of the defunct Imperial State Pottery of Vienna (1718–1861)," which suggests that they hoped gnomes would appeal to fashionable tastes. Elliott concluded with the opinion that by the 1990s, gnomes had ceased to be acceptable because of a revived disapproval of painted sculpture and it was this taste that was reflected in the RHS Chelsea Show Schedule, Article 15, which forbids "highly coloured figures, gnomes, fairies or any similar creatures, actual or mythical, for use as garden ornaments." However, while the gardening glitterati may snub the gnome, there are many people who couldn't imagine their gardens without them.

disneyfication of the gnome

Most of the early models of gnomes produced in Germany in the 19th century followed the "dwarf" concept. Although beautifully made, they mainly adhered to the heavy Victorian fashion; they were not brightly painted and did not portray the merry, smiling little man we expect to see today. This image of the gnome continued virtually unchanged until the 1930s when, in 1937, Walt Disney Productions created their animated film, *Snow White and the Seven Dwarfs*, based on the Brothers Grimm tale of *Little Snow White*. The story involves a wicked queen's attempt to have her stepdaughter murdered. Snow White escaped and was given shelter by seven dwarfs who live deep in the forest, where they work as miners. Disney adapted the Brothers Grimm story by taking out or changing the more gory passages, but he kept the dwarfs as miners. He invented delightfully cute characters for them, with appropriate names and endearing features —Doc, Grumpy, Happy, Sneezy, Bashful, Sleepy and Dopey (who did not, incidentally, have a beard). They became household favorites everywhere and probably changed the popular image of the gnome forever. However, it was not until after the Second World War that the gnome's appearance was changed. Colors brightened and makers started producing the gnome we now know and that was, by then, also becoming universally recognized as a "garden gnome."

Although the Scandinavian tradition of Christmas gnomes continued, the garden gnome began to enter the public consciousness as a colorful, cheerful character that would brighten many suburban gardens.

Above: A 19th-century illustration for the Brothers Grimm's *Little Snow White* story, before the Disneyfication of the gnomes.

Right: A vintage terra-cotta gnome made by a German company, Etruria, *c.* 1866.

Below: Modern gnomes modeled on the chirpy dwarfs in the Disney film, *Snow White and the Seven Dwarfs*.

Opposite page: A 19th-century Kellermeister gnome made by Etruria. Kellermeisters (masters of the cellar) were not garden gnomes, but rather guardians of wine and beer stores, hence the keys on his belt and the bottles in his arms.

Opposite page: **Six ceramic gnome musicians made by Heissner, Germany, in 1950.**

Below: **Clemens Spang's fishing gnome, with music box fitted in base, 1950s.**

The Second World War had brought an end to most, if not all, production of ceramic gnome figures. Limited production resumed after the war, then, in 1960, the Zeho Plastic Company produced the first plastic garden gnome manufactured in Germany. Their gnomes followed the Disney style and were promoted as shatterproof and weatherproof, as opposed to the traditional fragile ceramic figures. Within a short time, plastic gnomes were dominating the market as other manufacturers, such as Heissner, brought out their plastic models and the garden gnome began to enjoy what was probably its most popular period. Influenced by the Disney image, manufacturers not only created these gnomes with softer features and made them look cute, they expanded the range of the gnome's "activities" to include fishing, gardening, playing musical instruments, and there were even sporty gnomes. These brightly colored characters became very popular as a garden decorations in many countries during the so-called "innocent 50s," but gradually they began to earn a reputation for being kitsch in the groovy 60s and swinging 70s. In the U.K. they were even thought to adversely affect the value of a house, and housesellers were advised "to hide them behind the begonias until the signature is on the dotted line."

Right, top: **A modern-day plastic resin Chinese gnome.**

Right, bottom: **Ceramic gnome by Philipp Griebel.**

In 1976, another image of the gnome was created by
Rien Poortvliet (1932–1995), the Dutch painter and
illustrator. His whimsical concept of gnomes followed
the mythological tradition and he saw them as
diminutive, stout beings, wearing tall, pointed,
conical hats and dressed in colors such as blue, red
or green; the male gnome always having a long white
beard. Poortvliet was an accomplished artist, usually
painting in watercolors, and he was particularly
well-known for his animals and nature scenes.
When he collaborated with the writer Wil Huygen to
create their famous *Gnomes* book, a fictional
guidebook to the mythical creatures, Poortvliet's
illustrations always showed his gnomes with the
ubiquitous conical hat. The book has seen an
astonishing number of reprints in several languages
and when the gnomes were subsequently modeled
by Egbert A. Hengelmolen as polyresin figures, the
"Poortvliet gnomes" were soon in demand
worldwide. There was a television series, *The World
of David the Gnome*, and variations of the Poortvliet
gnome figures have also been copied by a number of
other manufacturers. Originals are still much sought
after. A museum of Poortvliet's work was opened in
1992 in the Dutch town of Middelharnis, but
unfortunately had to close in 2006.

Czech, Polish and Far Eastern manufacturers also
began to mass-produce plastic resin garden gnomes,
and very often the Disney concept was even more
closely followed. However, the few remaining
ceramic gnome manufacturers in German stayed
loyal to the pre–Second World War models.

Although plastic resin gnomes now dominate the
scene, ceramic gnomes continue to be produced,
albeit on a reduced scale.

So where are the girls?

The female gnome was unheard of before the 1960s. Up until that time gnomes had always been portrayed as little old men with long white beards smoking pipes, or as manual workers wielding spades, tools, wheelbarrows, and so on. The female gnome entered the arena slowly. One of the first female gnomes to appear was made in Germany about 1962 by the world-famous Heissner Company. Made in ceramic, she was a cute 12-inch (30 cm) tall girl holding a basket and wearing a blue dress over a white blouse. Draped from her shoulders was a cream shawl. Her pretty face was topped by, of course, the floppy traditional gnome's red hat.

Rien Poortvliet introduced his version of the lady gnome in his *Gnomes* book. He portrayed them as plump, cheerful and friendly figures who looked after the children. They wore traditional clothes with full-length skirts that were gathered at the waist and of course they always wore the famous conical red hat.

The 1990s saw female "naughty" gnomes being introduced. They were shown wearing suspender belts, fishnet stockings and very little else. They came in all sizes and colors and were very popular. Many people called them obscene and rude, which caused an uproar within the gnome fraternity and many gnome enthusiasts thought it was an insult to the much loved, innocent gnome.

In about 2004, Philipp Griebel, of Gräfenroda, Germany, the company reputed to have originated the garden gnome, produced a delightful female gnome in traditional German dress and given the name "Lady Roda." But even she ran foul of the "Association for the Protection of Gnomes' Rights" at a gnome conference in Germany, when it was argued that gnomes had always been "men only" and must remain so. Delegates were told that it was inconceivable that women could be involved when gnomes were symbols of friendliness and suburban tranquillity. It was even suggested that if gnomes were given wives, sex, with its attendant tensions, would be introduced!

Despite these objections, Griebel's ladies have continue to sell well and the so-called "naughty girls" are still available, with many more models added to the ever-increasing range. The "naughty" gnome ladies will probably never end up in the garden but if you look carefully, you will find them in an office, bar or behind a book on the bookshelf. One thing for sure is though they started life as a traditional helpmate for gnomes, they will soon assert their own personalities.

Opposite page: **A Rien Poortvliet gnome.**

Above: **Miniature resin Rien Poortvliet male and female gnomes.**

Below: **Lady Roda with a male companion.**

it's a gnome's world

If you can't love gnomes, then you can at least laugh at them. No longer just static garden ornaments, they can get involved in some bizarre adventures.

In 2001, the French film *Amelie* featured a globe-trotting gnome and generated a renewed interest in the characters, particularly among the younger generation, that many say resulted in the surge in gnomenapping, gnome liberation fronts and traveling gnomes. Amelie took her father's beloved gnome and handed it to a friend, a stewardess for an international airline, who took it with her and had it photographed against a backdrop of world-famous tourist locations. Amelie's confused father began to receive photographs, apparently from his beloved, but now jet-setting gnome. Eventually, the gnome returned home and Amelie's father followed his gnome's example and set off to see the world.

Soon after the release of this film, an English gnome was reported to have vanished from his garden, only to turn up again a year later complete with a suntan and a little suitcase covered with travel labels.

What of other gnomes? A series of what might be described as modern, naughty gnomes came onto the market in the 1990s. These distinctive characters are perhaps not all suitable for display in the garden and may not be to everyone's taste, but for those with a broad sense of humor, they can bring out a smile. But beware, left out in the garden, they can fall foul of the PC brigade who fail to see the funny side.

Below left: **Mobile Joe (MJ) and his cheeky mates designed by Zwergen Power.**

Below right: **Flashers in the park by Zwergen Power.**

Away from the naughty and on to the sporty—a range of soccer action gnomes was produced for the 2006 World Cup and one large supermarket chain claimed they were selling them at a rate of one every five seconds.

When Rien Poortvliet created his concept of the gnome in 1976, yet another friendly looking old man had emerged to join the gnome species. Today, there is a wide range of different garden gnomes to suit all tastes. Interest in gnomes has certainly gone up and down over the years. Gardeners and households in Germany, where they probably enjoy the greatest popularity, remain steadfast in their devotion to the little characters, but dedicated gnome lovers can still be found in most countries. Gnomes have captured the popular imagination as far afield as the United States, Canada, Europe and Australia. Furthermore, vintage gnomes have become collectible; they fetch high prices at auctions and there are avid collectors in many countries. The serious collector can still find beautifully sculpted vintage gnomes; old illustrations of gnomes and ceramics with gnome decoration are much sought after. Meanwhile, the hobby collector has a huge range to choose from at the lower end and those seeking a laugh or a joke can find a gnome for any occasion. Those simply seeking to cheer up their gardens have no limit in their choice of gnomes.

From California to Florida, from the Isle of Skye to the Falkland Islands, from Germany to Afghanistan, Australia and New Zealand—there really is a world of gnomes.

Left: Ceramic gnomes made in Germany for the 2006 FIFA World Cup by Zwergen Power.

Below: Vintage early 20th-century Ferdinand Maresch gnome.

Bottom: Plastic gnomes made by Heissner for the 2006 FIFA World Cup.

the gnome makers

a giant among gnomes

The village of Gräfenroda in the German state of Thüringia, claims to be the birthplace of the garden gnome. A young boy, Philipp Griebel, born in Gräfenroda, was apprenticed to Heinrich Dornheim, a ceramic maker in the village. He went on to found his own factory in 1874 making, in common with other local ceramic producers, a variety of terra-cotta figures including animals such as deer, wolves, sheep and birds. Soon after this, Griebel began to produce

Left: The original "Wendelin" gnome was created by Wendelin Griebel in 1926. Only a few copies were made and production ceased in 1939. It was not until 2006 that the gnome was produced again, in limited numbers, by Philipp Griebel.

the gnome figures. At about the same time, August Heissner, another key figure in the gnome makers' hall of fame and who also had a factory in the area, began to produce gnomes. Much of this early history is based on a newspaper article from 1893, which described and illustrated the ceramic industry in Gräfenroda. Both Griebel and Heissner are generally accepted as the creators of the garden gnome as we know it, however, as you'd expect with these mythical little figures, there are possible contradictions.

In 1847, Sir Charles Isham, of Lamport Hall, United Kingdom, returned from a visit to Nuremburg with a collection of about 20 gnomes. He has the honorable status of being the first person in England to have gnomes living in their garden (see page 42). Additionally, in 1886, a company named Etruria in Neuwedell, which is now in Poland, was advertising high-quality gnomes for sale.

Griebel's gnomes, like those made by other manufacturers at the time, were in the image of the

Left: Philipp Griebel, recognized as one of the creators of the garden gnome.

Opposite page: A 15-year-old Willi Griebel being taught his craft by his father, Wendelin, in 1935.

miners who had once worked in the region. He created them with their distinctive red hats designed to protect their neck and shoulders from loose stones, their working clothes, their lantern and wheelbarrow or basket. His fine gnomes were exhibited at the Leipzig Fair in 1884. They sold well and were soon extremely well-traveled gnomes, being exported to all parts of the world. He is known to have been dealing directly with companies in London. At its peak, the Griebel factory produced about 300 different gnome characters in a variety of sizes.

Philipp Griebel's company continued to prosper under his son, Wendelin, but production was interrupted during the world wars and probably reached its lowest point after the Second World War and the political division of Germany. Wendelin's son, Willi Griebel, was managing the factory when Thüringia became part of the German Democratic Republic (East Germany) where, in 1948, the Ministry of Economic Affairs banned production of garden gnomes because they were deemed "not to fit into a socialist society," although limited and controlled production was later permitted for export. In 1972, the factory was nationalized and became part of the VEB Terrakotta Gräfenroda Company.

Meanwhile, in 1950, Wendelin's other son, Erich Griebel, had moved to Stuttgart where, in 1954, he was able to start a factory under his own name producing ceramic figures and traditional garden gnomes from original models. In 1957 he moved to the village of Rot am See in Baden-Württemburg,

where production continued. Erich's son, Günter Griebel, and his wife Jutta, carried on in the family gnome business as Der Zwergenkaufhaus until it closed in 2001.

the gnome makers

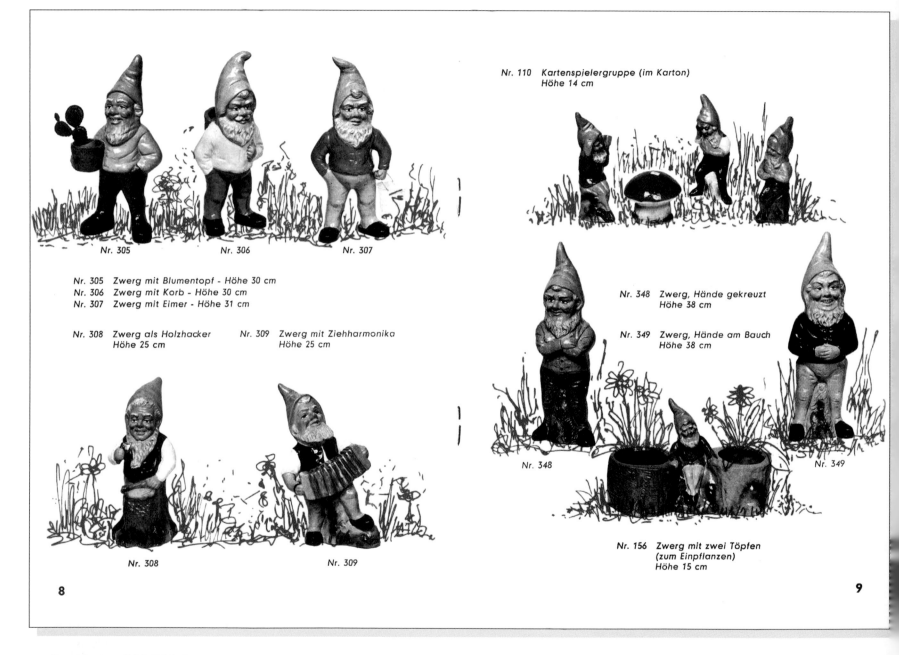

Nr. 305   Zwerg mit Blumentopf - Höhe 30 cm
Nr. 306   Zwerg mit Korb - Höhe 30 cm
Nr. 307   Zwerg mit Eimer - Höhe 31 cm

Nr. 308   Zwerg als Holzhacker   Nr. 309   Zwerg mit Ziehharmonika
           Höhe 25 cm   Höhe 25 cm

Nr. 110   Kartenspielergruppe (im Karton)
           Höhe 14 cm

Nr. 348   Zwerg, Hände gekreuzt
           Höhe 38 cm

Nr. 349   Zwerg, Hände am Bauch
           Höhe 38 cm

Nr. 156   Zwerg mit zwei Töpfen
           (zum Einpflanzen)
           Höhe 15 cm

8

9

Pages from an Erich Griebel
catalog *c*. 1955.

Nr. 105

Nr. 103

Nr. 100   Zwerge - Höhe 15 cm
3 Stück sort.

Nr. 102

Nr. 104

Nr. 351
Zwerg mit Angel
Höhe 10 cm

Nr. 103   Zwerg sitzend   -   Höhe 12 cm
Nr. 105   Zwerg mit Eimern -   Höhe 15 cm
Nr. 102   Zwerg liegend   -   Länge 14 cm
Nr. 104   Zwerg mit Karre   -   Höhe 15 cm

Nr. 302   Zwerg mit Sense - Höhe 28 cm

Nr. 101
Zwerg als Schaukler
Höhe 14 cm

Nr. 229
Zwerg als Schaukler
Höhe 25 cm

Nr. 225

Nr. 225a

Zwerg liegend links - Länge 22 cm

liegend rechts - Länge 20 cm

Nr. 151   Zwerg auf Korb - Höhe 12 cm

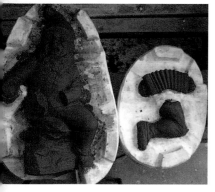

Top: **Reinhard Griebel pours clay into a mold.**

Above and right: **The pieces are assembled to make a gnome, and then cleaned.**

Top center: **The gnome in the kiln.**

On April 1, 1990, following German reunification, the gnome came home. Willi Griebel's son, Reinhard, still under the family company name "Philipp Griebel," and using original patterns and molds, resumed production of traditional, high-quality ceramic garden gnomes, which are generally recognized as the "Gräfenroda gnome." Today, the company is the only ceramic manufacturer remaining in Gräfenroda where signs proudly declare the town to be *Geburtsort der Gartenzwerge*—"Birthplace of the Garden Gnome." Adjacent to the factory is a small museum that exhibits old and new gnomes.

Helped by his wife, Iris, Reinhard fashions the little figures by hand and gives them all names such as Baldwin, Anton, Max, Heinz and many others.

Using local Thüringian clay, which he mixes with his own ingredients, Reinhard creates a slurry that is poured into a plaster mold made from the original patterns handed down from father to son. Surplus clay is poured back out and the remainder allowed to set before the mold is taken apart.

The new gnome is taken out of the mold and left to dry and, if in parts, assembled. It is rubbed down and polished to remove seams and blemishes before being placed in the kiln and baked at a temperature of 1980°F (1080°C).

When the gnome has cooled, it is ready for painting. First the gnome's face and beard are painted, giving it its unique character, then the clothing and, last, but not least, the red hat. Finally the gnome is varnished. A perfectly crafted garden gnome is now ready to be packed and sent on its travels to take up residence and pride of place in a new home.

Opposite page, top right: **After firing, the gnome is painted by a skilled porcelain painter and finally glazed.**

Right: **Herbert in his garden.**

other principal makers

Left: **A classic Bernhard Bloch gnome (1850–1899).**

In the late 19th and early 20th centuries there were at least 16 companies, with many skilled craftsmen, producing high-quality ceramic gnome figures in the Gräfenroda district, and several more in the general region of southeast Germany and Czechoslovakia. Below are the stories of some of the principal manufacturers at that time.

Bernhard Bloch

Some of the finest gnome figures were produced during the late 1800s in Eichwald, Bohemia (now Dubi in the Czech Republic), a small village created by a 15th-century group of miners and set among deep oak forests. In 1895, a flourishing ceramics factory in the village was sold to Bernhard Bloch, then a prosperous ceramics entrepreneur from Germany, and it continued production as the Eichwald Porcelain and Stove Factory, Bloch & Co. The range of their products is somewhat intriguing— they were particularly well known for manufacturing smoker's accoutrements such as thermodores, but also earthenware gnome figures. Most of the figures were marked on the base with the letters "BB," together with a model number.

The company was nationalized after the Second World War and amalgamated with other local pottery and porcelain makers to form the Duchov Porcelain Company.

Goebel

The company was founded by Franz and William Goebel. They discovered the artwork of Berta Hummel when she was a Franciscan nun and, by arrangement with her convent, they gained the right to create three-dimensional models based on her work. The first Hummel figurines were produced in 1935 and Sister Hummel worked with the company to create new products. She died in 1946 but her influence on the company remained and the genuine Hummel figures are still sold worldwide. The figures have become a highly popular collectible; even comedian Jerry Seinfeld mentioned them in his stand-up act. If you want to take the stress out of what to buy relatives at Christmas, just start them off on a Hummel collection. That will be Christmas all wrapped up for quite a few years.

Between 1971 and 1987, Goebel produced its "Co-Boy" gnome figurines. There are more than 60 models, patterned on different human professions and activities such as doctors, lawyers, athletes, cooks, and so on. Like all the company's products, they are noted for their beautiful style and excellent craftsmanship. These 6-inch (15 cm) gnomes are now very collectible and if you have a friend who is a doctor, lawyer, etc., that's their birthday present taken care of.

Right: **Brum, the gnome lawyer. Made by Goebel, he stands 6 inches (15 cm) tall and is part of the Co-Boy range.**

Eckardt & Mentz

Information on this company is very limited, but it is known that they were one of the oldest ceramic gnome manufacturers in Gräfenroda. They were in production from the late 19th century until 1945 and their craftsmanship was of the highest order. Made from terra-cotta clay, examples of their gnome figures are now very rare. So, if you're lucky enough to have an Eckardt & Mentz gnome, make sure that your other gnomes take care of it.

Hans Groth

Hans Groth produced ceramic gnomes during the 1950s in Lauterbach, Hessen, in central Germany, under the tradename of Purzel Ceramics. His gnomes were generally naively modeled and have distinctive large eyes.

Above right: Eckardt & Mentz gnomes from a Gräfenroda catalog, *c.* 1900.

Right: A typical Purzel gnome made in Germany in 1957.

August Heissner

August Heissner began producing garden gnomes in around 1870. His idea was to create products that would bring people joy and relaxation. Could he have ever imagined that one day gnomes would be traveling the world, sending postcards to their owners or starring in movies? Together with Philipp Griebel, he is acknowledged as one of the original creators of the garden gnome. Made exclusively out of clay and lovingly handpainted, his gnomes were exported throughout Europe and then later the world.

The Heissner company was brought to a standstill by the two World Wars. In 1949 the company moved to the town of Lauterbach, Hessen. There was a renaissance for the garden gnome and the company began to prosper again. The 1960s saw the introduction of cheap plastic gnomes and Heissner survived by taking on the competition and introducing their own range of brightly colored plastic figures. They have continued to make plastic gnomes but are now better known as a leading producer of pond and garden equipment.

Left: **An early Heissner gnome *c.* 1939, now living at the Devon Gnome Reserve.**

Right: **Twenty-first-century Heissner gnome made from PVC plastic.**

31

Right: **A highly collectible and therefore valuable** *c.* **1900 classic Maresch gnome.**

Opposite page: **Ferdinand Maresch gnomes shown in a** *c.* **1900 catalog.**

Johann Maresch

Johann Maresch, a German, was born in 1821 and by the age of 20 was in partnership with Adolph Baehr who owned a factory producing ceramic wares in Usti nad Labem, in what is now the Czech Republic. Adolph died in 1849 but Johann continued the business, producing an extensive range of top-quality porcelain and ceramic figures, gnomes and other kinds of fairytale characters and animals for the home and garden. In fact, the factory was one of the first to mass-produce gnomes that, usually marked "JM," were unequaled and, by the beginning of the 20th century, were being exported all over Europe.

The business continued to prosper under Johann's son Ferdinand, who took over in 1890, exporting a wide range of high-quality ceramics throughout Europe and to North America. Production continued until the Second World War when the factory was bombed. Post-war days were very difficult. The German population was expelled from the border regions of Czechoslovakia, the factory was nationalized and not enough skilled workers remained. Demand dropped substantially and the factory closed in 1948.

Vintage Maresch gnomes in good condition are now rare. They are much sought after and always sell for good prices at auctions.

Nr. 6360   59 cm   Nr. 6361   60 cm   Nr. 6362   59 cm   Nr. 6363   59 cm   Nr. 6364   60 cm

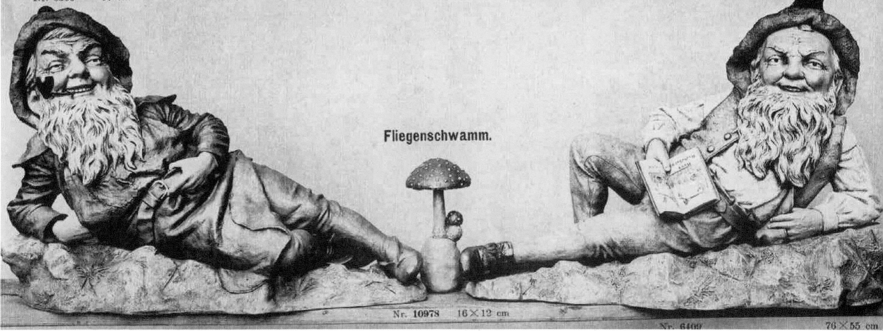

Fliegenschwamm.

Nr. 10978   16 × 12 cm

Nr. 6409   76 × 55 cm

Louis Romeiss

Louis Romeiss, like so many other gnome makers, was located in Gräfenroda, Thüringia, where they made outstanding gnomes until 1986, many of which have become collector's items. Made of finely sculptured earthenware and handpainted, some of their gnomes were not marked, but are distinguishable by the fine facial features and relatively oversized hat.

Kurt Renno

Kurt Renno manufactured ceramic gnomes during the 1950s in a small workshop in Ransbach, Westerwald, Germany, under the trade name "Reju." Reju gnomes were substantial and heavy, made of red clay and terra cotta and were stamped with the trademark "Re."

Plachy & Materne

One of the earliest German makers of plastic gnomes, Plachy & Materne of Wirges, Westerwald, Germany, started producing garden ornamentation such as gnomes, animals and toadstools under the name of Puma Plastics during the 1960s. Their gnomes were made of hard plastic, blown in two-part molds and then handpainted. They manufactured and exported the gnomes extensively during the period 1965–1968.

Their trade leaflets, brochures and catalogs show a large range of gnomes that were available during this period of early plastic models. Europe could not get enough of them and business boomed. One can only imagine the effect this huge population of gnomes must have had on garden design during this time.

34

Zeho

In 1960, Zeho was the first German company to produce plastic garden gnomes. Their gnomes were made in hard plastic with distinctively cheerful faces and were marked "Zeho West Germany." Gnomes are still being manufactured under the name "Zeho Germany."

Clemens Spang

Clemens Spang made fine gnomes in Ludwigsburg, Germany, in the 1950s and 60s. His gnomes generally came with teeth showing and parted legs, which has become a rare feature in models of that era (parted legs made the gnomes fragile in transit and makers gradually began to favor stronger figures, filling in the gap between the legs with grass or a tree stump). They are very recognizable by their not-so-cute, cheeky faces and floppy caps. They were made of sturdy earthenware and were partly spray-painted and then handpainted and varnished. The company was in business for only a short time and little is known about Clemens Spang himself.

Left: **Two happy gnomes— one by Clemens Spang (*top left*) and the other by Zeho.**

35

in the U.S.

Right: **A cast iron gnome that is thought to be made by a Kankakee foundry.**

Germany was the main producer of gnomes in the 19th and 20th centuries and the popularity of their gnomes quickly spread. Gnomes were exported to the United States, opening up a huge new market. Many of the gnomes were copied and some U.S. companies began making their own models.

Iron foundries in the Kankakee area of Illinois are known to have made a variety of domestic items such as heavy doorstops in the early 1900s, but among their more whimsical products were large, cast iron gnomes. They would have been an expensive garden ornament in their day and only a few have survived. One, for example, with something of a wry smile on his face, is still lighting the way to a home in Kalamazoo.

While traditional ceramic gnome manufacturing has almost disappeared in Europe, with Philipp Griebel being the last company still in production in Gräfenroda, the skills are being strongly revived in the United States where the likes of Candice Kimmel, Brian Kibler, Tom Clark and Sam Girton are continuing to produce high-quality figures.

Candice Kimmel

Artist Candice Kimmel has brought her love of old-world garden gnomes from her native country of Wales to the gardens of the United States. Her studio is located in the beautiful Black Hills of South Dakota. In a modern world of concrete and plastic, Candice Kimmel's gnomes are handmade and cast from her own original sculptures and from rare 19th- and 20th-century antique gnomes.

"When beginning a sculpture," Candice says, "I have an idea of what the gnome will look like but the gnome never turns out the way I envision it, and I'm always surprised by the mysterious characters that 'appear' out of the clay."

Each gnome takes between one and two weeks to complete and because of the handmade and handglazed process, no two gnomes are exactly alike—each one is unique. Fired in English stoneware pottery, which has a lovely quality and feel, and with a finish that ensures they are weather resistant, Kimmel gnomes will last for generations and can be displayed with pride.

Above: "Merry Weather," a 2002 Kimmel gnome.

Left: Herbert, a reproduction Heissner gnome made by Kimmer gnomes.

37

the gnome makers

Brian Kibler

Above: **Brian Kibler, with one of his Maresch gnomes.**

Right: **One of Brian Kibler's Maresch reproductions.**

Brian Kibler, a New York artist, was inspired by Maresch gnomes whose reputation had long survived the end of their production. Intrigued by the mischievous little figures, Brian uses his talents as a mold maker to recast original Johann Maresch statues, which he acquires whenever he can. "I give these wonderful gnomes a second life to live outside in the garden where they were meant to be." Often, the original Maresch gnomes that Brian obtains are deteriorating. "They probably served a lifetime in the garden so they show signs of wear," says Brian, adding, "I only hope I look so good at 150."

So with a passion that goes beyond the ordinary, Brian recasts these intricate little figures in his New York studio. He pours rubber around the original gnomes to form a detailed mold and he then casts in a variety of materials, his favorites being plastic and cement. "I find myself casting more and more in cement because I find the ties it has with garden statuary more appealing, plus the quality of the paint on the cement is simply extraordinary."

"I know several collectors of Maresch's work and over the years I have seen pieces fetch amazing prices," Brian says. "I wanted to be able to make these fascinating garden statues more accessible." These gnomes have come a long way, from the former Czechoslovakia to a studio in New York.

Brian's work has been recognized by the Museum of Usti nad Labem in the Czech Republic who honored him by including his gnomes in an exhibition celebrating the work of Johann and Ferdinand Maresch and their factory.

Tom Clark

Tom Clark, a doctor of divinity, left his academic life to devote his time to sculpture and what could be described as "the gnome business" in 1985. He is now famous for his creation of gnomes, woodspirits and leprechauns, many of which are modeled on real characters. His casting process severely limits the mold life and reduces the number of castings, and thus each model becomes a limited edition. His work, made in the Cairn Studio in Davidson, North Carolina, is now highly collectible and it is thought that there are more than 50 clubs across the United States formed solely for the collection and trading of Tom Clark's gnomes.

Sam Girton

A Democrat and Professor of Visual Communications at Ohio University, Sam Girton produces a series of gnomes modeled on President George W. Bush—see pages 119–20 for more.

Left: **Mugmom (1984) by the Tom Clark Cairn Studio.**

great gnome collections

Collecting gnomes has been, and continues to be, a passion for many people in many different countries. These collections range from the exquisitely small to the fabulously large. The Lamport Hall and Friar Park gnome collections in England are perhaps among the most famous, but many other people across the world love their gnomes and have, in several instances, gathered significant collections of gnomes and gnome ephemera. It is not possible to give space to all of these collectors, but some of them have shown such dedication to the little folk that they cannot go without some mention.

lampy's home

Lamport Hall in Northamptonshire, United Kingdom, was bought by John Isham in 1560. It remained in the Isham family for the next 416 years, during which time it was developed and redesigned, and it expanded into the quintessential classic English country estate it is today. The family amassed a wonderful collection of books, furniture, paintings and rare antiques, and in 1976, the 12th Baronet of Lamport bequeathed the estate and its contents to the Lamport Hall Trust for the benefit of the nation. Its architecture and vast collection make Lamport Hall a national treasure, but possibly the most unusual item in that collection, and probably its most famous, must be Lampy, the garden gnome.

Gnomes, in one form or another, have had a place in English gardens for more than 150 years, although the term "garden gnome" was not in common use until about 1930. They are thought to have first appeared in England sometime after 1847 when Sir Charles Isham, the 10th baronet, an eccentric spiritualist who had inherited his mother's love of gardening, created a remarkable rockery in the grounds of the hall. It rose like a ruined castle, was 24 feet (7 m) tall and was the earliest example of a rock garden in England. It contained a wealth of unusual miniature plants, trees and shrubs, and he went on to populate it with 20 gnome figurines he brought back from Nuremburg, Germany. These are thought to have been the first garden gnomes displayed in England. Such figurines were sold in Germany at that time as ornaments for the house and it was Sir Charles's idea to use them outdoors.

For the rest of his life, Sir Charles personally attended to the rockery on a daily basis. He built a new wing onto the house, in which his bedroom overlooked the rockery so as to enable him to keep an ever-watchful eye on his "little people." To him, they were real people and he arranged them in tableaux of coal, crystal and diamond mines of his creation. A photograph of the gnomes displayed in this way was published in *The Gardeners' Chronicle* in 1897 (see photograph below). However, his daughters are thought to have had the gnomes removed after he died in 1903 because they had never liked them. Then, in 1976, when the rockery was being restored, a single 6-inch (15 cm) tall gnome was found hidden in a crevice. He had survived and today, Lampy, as he is known, is a prized exhibit in Lamport Hall. If you would like to meet Lampy personally, the house and garden are open to the public.

Below: **Late 19th-century photograph of Sir Charles Isham's gnome rockery.**

Left: Lampy, the only
surviving Lamport Hall
gnome and a much respected
elder of the gnome world.

43

with a little help from my gnomes

Above: **The iconic album cover photograph for** *All Things Must Pass* **was taken by Barry Feinstein and featured the recently recovered Friar Park gnomes.**

A second significant collection of gnomes to be displayed in an English garden was created in 1896, when Sir Frank Crisp, a rich London lawyer, built the 120-room Friar Park at Henley-on-Thames. The park was built in a mixture of French Renaissance and Gothic architectural styles, with an extensive garden featuring three lakes. The garden was divided into a number of different areas, including an Elizabethan-style garden and an enormous rock garden. Within the rock garden he erected a 29-foot (9 m) model of the Matterhorn, built from about 7,000 tons of Yorkshire stone and topped with a piece of rock allegedly from the summit of the actual mountain. He completed it with a herd of cast iron chamois goats.

44

There were underground caves connected by a river and the caves were adorned with items such as skeletons and mirrors. In the caves and grounds of the house he also placed, what must have been by any measure, the consummate collection of about 100 large, German-made, terra cotta gnomes, which are thought to have been supplied by the Wahliss Galleries in London.

The house was later used as a convent and a school for many years, and then in 1970, Friar Park became the home of George Harrison of The Beatles. He recorded his album *All Things Must Pass* that year and it includes the *Ballad of Sir Frankie Crisp (Let It Roll)*, a song in homage to the creator of the house.

The album was very successful, outselling some of The Beatles' albums and reached number one on both sides of the Atlantic. The cover for that album is now regarded as an iconic image of George Harrison and gnomes were a large part of it.

Right: **Some of the gnomes in the *All Things Must Pass* photograph are 19th-century Ferdinand Maresch gnomes.**

great gnome collections

Below: **A Ferdinand Maresch gnome resting casually.**

Photographer Barry Feinstein remembers the session at Friar Park to shoot the pictures for that album cover. The gardens were being renovated and "we photographed for days." Barry says of the session, "Then someone called George and told him that the gnomes that were stolen from Friar Park could be bought back. They asked him if he wanted to buy them. He said 'Sure.' They brought them back and they were laid out on the lawn. We went out and looked at them and I said, 'There's the cover.' We didn't have to move a thing. In about two minutes, we had the cover. It was spontaneous."

Barry Feinstein's famous photograph shows four gnomes of an unusually large size, lying as a group around George. These large figures are about 3 feet (1 m) long and such gnomes are known to have been made by only a few manufacturers. Some of the gnomes in the photograph can in fact be identified from a late 19th-century catalog as the work of Ferdinand Maresch in Usti nad Labem, Czechoslovakia.

Another of George Harrison's albums features a photograph of the famous gnomes of Friar Park. *Thirty three and ⅓rd* was released in 2004 in a remastered format and the CD case booklet contains a photograph of George and his father, Harry, at Friar Park surrounded by nine large standing and reposing gnomes. What a privilege to have your photo taken with a Beatle, and twice at that! Again, some of the gnomes are clearly from the Maresch factory.

Griebel, Heissner and Maresch catalogs from around 1900 show that some of these large gnomes were made not just as garden ornaments, but were also meant to stand as gate or door guardians, with a "Portier" badge on their hat ("portier" is of French origin and means "gatekeeper"). In 2007, an antique dealer in Cowbridge, South Wales, took in a fine "Portier" gnome, which had been acquired in Builth Wells, Mid Wales in 2006. It is very similar to one of the gnomes on George Harrison's right in the *Thirty three and ⅓rd* photograph and is from the same factory. Some damage can be seen on the Friar Park gnome, which also does not have a staff, and there seem to be some color differences with the Welsh gnome. Have these two friends been missing each other all this time? It would not have been unusual to see such gnomes standing at the side of a door or gate into a large house. Not many of these gnomes would have been made and they would have been expensive—in fact a 19th-century German advertisement priced them at 90 Marks, at a time when a farm laborer's wages for a whole year would have been about 50 Marks.

So, it seems that the gnomes of Friar Park provided George with a little inspiration on more than one occasion. Now, that's quite a claim to fame.

Left: A 3-foot (1 m) terra cotta "Portier" gnome identical to the one photographed with George Harrison at Friar Park.

a garden for george

Why a garden for George? Well, Allison Devine had two lifelong passions. One was for George Harrison of The Beatles, the other was for gardening. Both started in 1967.

In February 2005, having moved to a house with gardens that were in need of some tender loving care, she faced the monumental challenge of redesigning the garden from scratch. At this stage she wasn't really thinking about having a themed garden; she just wanted something low maintenance, that looked good all year round and contained plants she liked.

Due to unforeseen delays in finalizing the purchase of the new house, Allison found she had plenty of spare time on her hands to plan the garden, or in reality, gardens. Being on a corner plot, there were three very separate planting areas, each one a garden in its own right. The soil tended toward the acidic that pleased Allison, as she adores rhododendrons and they require acidic soil to thrive. She started surfing the Internet, looking for suppliers of these beautiful, showy shrubs. While looking through one online catalog, she noticed that there were dwarf rhododendrons named after each of Snow White's Seven Dwarfs. Allison called her husband to the computer with the words, "I know you'll think I'm crazy but…"

It didn't take long to explain the idea. When George Harrison passed away in December 2001, Allison was moved by some of the wonderful tributes. If people could theme their gardens around a fairy story, what was to stop her using George Harrison—musician,

gardener, humanitarian and resident of Friar Park (see page 44), as her inspiration? He had inspired her in so many things since the tender age of 4¾, which was also about the age at which she started to take an interest in her father's lifelong passion for gardening. What better personal tribute could she create? Allison's husband gave her the smile he always reserves for when she suggests something "crazy." He expressed his doubts; not about the idea itself, but about whether she would be able to find enough plants that would fit the theme.

Allison posted her idea on the message board at George Harrison's official website and she received a huge amount of encouragement. Many people were soon making suggestions, not just about plants but about other features to include. One very recurrent theme was gnomes. George had been pictured with the Friar Park gnomes for two of his albums and he had included real-life representations of the gnomes in the video for *Crackerbox Palace*.

March and April were spent browsing plant catalogs looking for "George connections." She decided that not only would she choose plants that in some way had a connection via their variety name, but also plants that George himself had grown or mentioned in interviews. Allison started buying plants, but more importantly, she recruited gnomes to live in the garden. She soon had quite a collection, all carefully wrapped and packed ready to be taken to their new home.

Allison and her husband moved into their house in late May. What greeted her in the garden stopped her in her tracks. The "large shrub" at the end of the garden revealed itself to be a mixture of shoulder-high stinging nettles, brambles and ground elder. For the first time Allison felt daunted by the amount of work involved and her heart sank. She wanted the garden to be so right. After all, this was to be her tribute to George and she had all the gnomes to make a home for. Then something flashed into her mind; in an interview George had described the gardens at Friar Park as being choked by brambles when he moved in. Suddenly she knew she could rise to the challenge just as he had done.

Allison got to work clearing the stinging nettles and she couldn't believe what was revealed. There was a small, raised bed and tucked right at the back was a wooden wishing well and a long-forgotten and somewhat sad-looking gnome! Allison remembered that George had discovered the gnomes of Friar Park hidden away when he started work on the house and gardens, so this spurred her on to work even harder. The gnome that she discovered beneath the nettles was given the name Noddy—he originally had a nodding head but the mechanism was rusty and so he doesn't nod very well anymore.

Opposite page: **One of Allison Devine's favorite gnomes, who tends her Penny Lane climbing rose.**

Right: **Noddy, the first gnome resident.**

By the beginning of July, the layout of the garden had been completed and plants added. Allison had plants with variety names such as "Cloud Nine," "Olivia," "Patty B," "Ringo," "The Beatles," "McCartney," "Strawberry Fields," and she even managed to find a rare alpine auricula called "George Harrison." Allison also planted several Japanese acers, because Dhani Harrison spoke of George's father planting them at Friar Park, as well as plants George himself had mentioned as "good plants to grow" in a Web chat in February 2001.

Noddy lives at the bottom of the garden, near the spot where he was found, but now he is among the miscanthus and bamboo and has the company of a diminutive pal called Dennis. Dennis is so small he is jokingly referred to as "a test pilot for Airfix." All of the other gnomes have been given names—among them Ying and Yang, who were donated by Allison's parents, and two characters who look like friars. These are named Frankie and Crisp.

Not all of the gnomes live in the garden itself. Some are in pots and containers and one even has the comfort of being indoors. He is a "George Harrison" gnome from a set of four depicting the Beatles and was a housewarming gift from a friend.

The beauty of any garden is that it is never finished and even now, more than two years later, Allison still finds plants to include in the planting scheme. She has redesigned all three gardens but there is one garden that she enjoys the most—that garden where

the gnomes live. She spends her time thinking about George and chatting to the little residents as she works. The gnomes work hard too and are often heard to mutter, "It's been a hard day's night!"

Just as George dedicated his autobiography to "Gardeners Everywhere," Allison has dedicated her garden to George. You can view more of the garden at www.garden-for-george.com where Allison says, "Thank you, George, for being my inspiration."

The entire project is Allison's personal tribute to George and it is not endorsed in any way by the Harrison family or estate.

Opposite page: **The gnome in charge of watering the plants.**

Left: **Two gnomes called Ying and Yang.**

Above: **Allison's very special George Harrison gnome.**

a magical place

Across Europe there are many collections of gnomes of every size, shape and style, but none have the diversity that can be seen at The Gnome Reserve. The reserve is located within 4 acres (1.2 ha) of beautiful grounds in rural countryside between Bideford and Bude, 7 miles (11 km) from the Devon/Cornwall border in England.

The founder of the reserve, Ann Atkin, and her husband, Ron, are both prize-winning graduates of the Royal Academy of Arts, London. Ann had previously studied at Brighton College of Art and Ron at Loughbrough College of Art. They moved into The Old Rectory near West Putford, Devon, with their family in 1971 and started collecting gnomes in 1978. This was partly due to having been inspired by Goethe's poem *Herman und Dorothea* and

Opposite page left: **Ann Atkin, founder of the Devon Gnome Reserve.**

Opposite page right: **Gnomes at work, rest and play.**

Right: **The more precious gnomes live in this glass house.**

Erasmus Darwin's epic poem *The Botanic Garden*, but the one secret that Ann will not divulge is precisely why she started The Gnome Reserve. She will just say that, "Gnomes became very important to me and I wanted to share them with people. I wanted to do my bit towards the re-greening of our planet, to give people a new angle on seeing, a way for each person, regardless of age, to see everything in nature as if for the first time and to be astonished by it."

There are now more than 2,000 gnomes living in the Devon grounds, although the old, rare and more fragile ones are kept in sheltered accommodation or,

55

as it is known, The Museum. Vintage gnomes dating back to the 19th century can be found in The Museum but the exact number of gnomes in the reserve as a whole can only be guessed at because, according to Ann, "they come and go." She says she often finds that new gnomes have arrived after visitors have left for the day.

The reserve is laid out in a variety of habitats for the gnomes. In addition to the more traditional fairground, birthday party and fishing pond arrangements, as visitors wander around they will see an airport, a motorbike track, rock climbing, a rocket launcher as well as gnomes engaged in many other activities.

Below: **The gnome moto-cross.**

Opposite page: **Card-playing gnomes next to the wishing well.**

The Gnome Reserve opened in 1979 and Ann says she was delighted to have about 8,000 visitors that year. "I came to the conclusion that it must have been very embarrassing for the gnomes to have been stared at by so many people." It was then decided to loan gnome hats to visitors, so the gnomes would just think other gnomes had arrived! "Of course it was funny to see tiny babies, toddlers, children, parents and grandparents all strolling around the woodland wearing brightly colored pointed hats." She has always said that gnomes are 100 percent serious and 100 percent humor, so she was thrilled to hear people say that The Gnome Reserve is the happiest place they know on the planet. One couple said how delighted they were because it had stimulated their 2-year-old's imagination—a couple of days after his visit to the reserve, he told them he'd seen a gnome in their garden playing a violin. During the second and third years, and in the early 1980s, the reserve had about 30,000 visitors each season between March and the end of October, which was a lot to deal with. Visitor numbers are now slightly more manageable as there are more attractions in the local area.

Management of the reserve was taken over by Ann's son and daughter-in-law, Richard and Meg Atkin, in 1992. Richard and Meg live at the reserve with their two young sons, Mark and Joe, and they continue to add to the magical place and its wonderful atmosphere. Richard makes many of the gnomes that live in the woodland and others he sends to buyers around the world—his abseiling gnome is a favorite.

Meg's homemade cakes and cream teas are becoming legendary in themselves and she lovingly tends the Wild Flower Garden, much to Ann's delight. A local newspaper, the *North Devon Journal*, gave the reserve three full-color pages in 2007, one of them being a photograph of Joe with the reserve's GNASA gnomes. Needless to say, the "G" stands for "Gnome"! Joe's facial expression certainly seems to say, "Aren't I lucky to live here?"

Ann, who continues to take an active part in the reserve, says she sees some people return every year; they say their visit to Devon is incomplete unless they come to The Gnome Reserve. These frequent visitors often become friends. Some people return after a gap of a few years and enjoy seeing all the new additions; some add a gnome of their own to the collection every time they visit and some return to bring new generations of the family. "Probably everyone who comes, sees it differently," Ann says. "Certainly there is a lot of laughter. People forget any worries or problems in their everyday life and they can be seen breaking into a smile as they come up the drive and notice the first welcoming gnomes." People who have never met take photographs for each other and Ann is sure that a visit slows people down from the frantic speed of town and city life. They have time to stand and stare and then leave the reserve feeling refreshed.

The Gnome Reserve quickly became a great media attraction and it has appeared in over 60 TV programs, in addition to being featured on the radio and in newspapers, magazines and books. The Gnome Reserve also represented Britain "as a place to visit" in Tokyo's British Embassy publication *Britain 2000*. The reserve was given a large space for a photograph and description and put on the same page as Princess Anne. Harrods and Harvey Nichols stores only had a thumbnail-sized description! "Although filming, making advertisements, visiting celebrities, and unusual happenings are always highlights, it is usually the everyday enjoyment of sharing the place with people aged from 1 to 100 which is so wonderful," remarks Ann. One of the many great memories that sticks in her mind was watching in amazement as a sheik took off his head cloth and replaced it with a gnome hat.

Ann continues to paint, under her professional name, Ann Fawssett Atkin, and visitors can view her original watercolors and limited edition prints of landscapes, birds, butterflies, lakes, waterfalls, rainbows and sometimes gnomes and fairies, that are displayed for sale in The Gnome and Fairy Gallery at the entrance to the reserve, together with individually modeled pottery pixies, which Ann creates in her studio. (See also page 153 for an example of Ann's work.)

Left: **Abseiling gnomes.**

Opposite page: **There's plenty to keep the gnomes amused at The Gnome Reserve.**

gnome habitat U.S.A.

Liz lives in Auburn, California, with her husband and son on a 5-acre (2 ha) property on which they keep horses, chickens, geese, ducks and a Norwich terrier. They also belong to the local wildlife rescue association and help to rehabilitate injured or orphaned animals. She has been collecting gnomes since 1979. Here's the story of how her collection began.

In December 1979, Liz participated in a Christmas gift exchange at work. One of her co-workers, knowing that she had a fascination for the cover of the Rien Poortvliet and Wil Huygen book *Gnomes*, decided that the she would give Liz the book. "At that point in my life, I started looking for gnomes— and gnomes started looking for me!"

Not long after reading and then rereading the book, Liz was at Lake Tahoe for the weekend with her husband and his parents. They were in one of the casinos when Liz's mother-in-law spotted some Co-Boy miniature gnomes reduced in price in the gift shop. She bought Liz her first two gnomes—Bit the bachelor and Walter the jogger. The collection had begun! There were more Co-Boy gnomes to come and then Liz discovered Dr. Tom Clark's gnomes and of course she had to have some of his work (see page 39). Liz followed this by discovering the Artina line of gnomes, which were later produced by Flambro and then the Enesco Corporation.

Liz's nights were filled with online treasure hunts, learning about gnomes, tracking down gnomes she wanted and looking for places to buy gnomes.

Opposite page: Liz with a gang of gnomes.

Right: A display at the Gnome Museum.

Weekends were spent visiting garden centers, antique shops and antique fairs in search of gnome statuary. She always hoped to find old European figurines—through her research, Liz had become familiar with the names of all the German manufacturers and longed to have pieces of their handpainted terra-cotta work.

"There was something about the way a gnome looks," says Liz. "They called out to me from the very beginning." She saw them as short, childlike beings, but with old features, wrinkles and white hair. "It was the intrigue of the opposites. The more I learned about their personality and purpose, the deeper I fell in love with them and their way of life."

When Liz looks at a gnome, or pictures one in her mind, she says that they make her smile. They also make her think about her connection with Mother Earth. "They ask me to re-examine my life, my lifestyle and my relationships," she adds. "Gnomes are a happy and industrious group and always ready to share their wisdom and talents." For Liz, choosing a favorite gnome is as difficult as picking a favorite child. Each gnome comes from either a special person, place or artist, and holds memories.

Both pages: Gnomes from all walks of life live happily together in Liz's Gnome Museum.

gnome habitat u.s.a.

Liz has some very special gnomes in her collection that mark significant occasions or are rare, different or from limited editions. For example, Klaus Wickl made only 15 figurines from one of his castings for an Enesco retailer promotion and Liz has one of those. Ron Lee, an artist and sculptor who is known for his clown figurines, made four gnome figurines—Liz has two of the four, which is more than Ron's own museum possesses.

At a rough estimate, Liz has more than 2,000 pieces in her collection, which now includes scrimshaw, gnome jewelry, tableware, birdbaths, wind chimes, clothing, books, calendars, posters, stationery, candles, a gnome chess set, and so on and so on. The collection used to fit inside the house but every room was filled, so she had to find a new home. As a result, Gnome Habitat U.S.A. was created and the collection is now comfortably housed in a barn that has been converted into a gnome museum with a library upstairs.

There are a lot of gnomes living outside, too. Some on a little knoll, others under some shrubs—there are so many, the chickens and deer keep knocking them over despite every effort to secure them. Her outside gnomes also require maintenance as the sun fades the paintwork, so she is planning to use automotive paint to give them a longer life.

"I am sure I have gnome radar," says Liz. "I can pick out a red pointed hat in a 75,000 square foot antique mall within 10 minutes if there is one there to be adopted! At flea markets and garage sales, I can hone in on the little people with amazing results."

Friends and family are used to seeing all of Liz's gnomes and listening to her going on and on about them. At the time of writing, Liz has not yet shared her gnomes with her recently arrived neighbors, but, she says, eventually they will meet them. "I am sure they will think we are just a normal family, that is until they head up to the museum, then they will know that something is really different!" Most people, she thinks, don't understand why she has so many gnomes. The smile they bring to people's faces when they discover all of them is priceless.

Liz has traveled to England and visited the Gnome Reserve in Devon (see page 54). She thought it was a magical place; it cast a spell on her and it was the inspiration for her own museum. She has one other specific gnome ambition: she would love to take care of Lampy, the Lamport Hall gnome (see page 42).

Below and opposite page:
**Gnomes line the paths to
greet and welcome visitors to
the Gnome Habitat.**

gnome habitat u.s.a.

gnome man's land

Gnome Man's Land, in California, was started by Jean as the result of three unrelated inspirations. First, her mother had always kept a lovely rock garden; second, a trip to Disneyland in the 1960s, which had, and still does have, a ride called the Storybook Land Canal Boats, in which people ride in small boats floating along a canal with miniature villages, trees and storybook characters. Third and finally, a friend once had two adorable gnomes on her office desk and Jean thought they were just so cute. These three memories stayed in the back of her mind for many years before flourishing into the unique world she created when she established her own garden after she married.

Below: **Jean and Jim at their Gnome home.**

Opposite page: **Welcome to our world. This truly is Gnome Man's Land.**

gnome man's land

Welcome To
My Garden

January 25, 1976, marks the date when Jean began to create a rock garden in the yard of the home she shares in California with her husband, Jim. They hauled in topsoil that was used to make irregular-shaped planting areas lined with rocks, which had been gathered from ranches and creek beds owned by friends. Then succulents and assorted small plants, many of which were cuttings Jean's mother shared from her garden, were added. Three gnomes ordered from a mail order catalog were then set in place. They looked so attractive positioned next to several colorful miniature roses transplanted from elsewhere in the yard. Jim even installed a sprinkler system and colored lights for nighttime viewing. That was the start of a seemingly never-ending project that would ultimately grow and become an amazing work of art. It is an enchanted garden enjoyed not only by Jim and Jean, but also by so many others over the years.

The main garden was gradually extended until it had about 150 gnomes and just as many varieties of complementary mini roses. Meandering paths, covered with bark, provide a number of good spots for gnomes to congregate in storylike settings. There are many gnome fishermen who spend the majority of their time on the banks of a 16-foot (5 m) long dry creek that ambles through one section of the garden, and most of them have prize-winning fish dangling from their hooks! This is just one of countless mini themes found within this garden.

The Bunny Trail has numerous gnomes posed with little creatures and their carrot motif furniture. A picnic can be observed at the far end, where gnomes are drinking their favorite beverages while gathered around a little picnic table. Another is barbecuing something for their lunch and others are grouped together nearby to form a small band that appears to be playing a medley of happy tunes.

One area of this garden has some gnomes experiencing life country style. Theirs is a gated community with a few pigs standing behind a gate, guarding the entrance to their domain by only allowing chosen individuals to pass. A fiddling gnome practices as another mows a grassy patch. Others feed tamed bluebirds or pet a gaggle of geese.

The Rest Area is where you will find gnomes who are napping, quietly reading or appearing to slowly mosey around. A favorite pastime here is playing checkers, chess or cards. Outhouses built by Jean's late father for both the gnomes and gnomettes are at convenient locations. Arched bridges enable these little people to cross over from one territory to another.

A second gnome garden, the Gnome Gardener's Garden, parallels the main rock garden on the other side of the walkway. Some 48 gardening gnomes are usually in the area. They are cheerfully doing a wide range of chores with their hoes, shovels, wheelbarrows, spades, tractors and flower carts.

Top: **A band of merry gnome troubadours.**

Above: **Gnomes at work.**

Opposite page: **Gnome pastoral.**

69

The Forest Rock Garden evolved in 1990. It displays gnomes as woodcutters, mountain climbers and hunters. Gnomes also share this habitat with deer and bears they have befriended. Smokey Bear is in the center and seems to reign over this territory.

A Frog Garden was introduced to the collection in 1999, where gnomes and amphibians frolic together in delightful harmony among a double row of miniature roses beside a long fence. Some are on swings in a tree, above others bathing in a wooden barrel or bucket. Numerous gnomes are seen riding large frogs with turtles and rabbits also joining in the fun.

The largest gnome-populated development came about in 1999, in the Woodland Area. It is here that a seven-member, life-sized, deer family of statuary is in view. The 15-foot (4.5 m) swathe of thicket formed by redwood trees, shrubs and assorted bushes has allowed for a number of gnome vignettes to be formed across its lawn-edged front, sides and rear areas. Entire colonies of gnomes are hidden from easy sight in Redwood Hollow and Little Gnome Glen; you happen upon them by chance. Each vignette is based on a different theme and makes for numerous opportunities to show off gnomes of every description, interacting with members of their own clans and/or animals.

The Life-size Garden was brought into existence to show what gnomes look like in real life-size scale. According to legend, if a human is lucky enough to

see a real live gnome, its height would be somewhere between 5 and 7 inches (13 and 18 cm). This fuchsia-laden gentle rolling mound of soil is covered with diminutive gnomes busying themselves with their daily routines. A creek through one corner supplies the perfect waterway for a gnome canoeing in a boat-shaped leaf. Another paints a welcome sign, while one bravely rides the back of a huge butterfly up in the trees. Scores more gnomes are captivated with far too numerous activities to mention.

The most recent gnome-themed addition to the garden is that of Dragonfly Way. Flowerpots with a wide range of greenery and flowering plants line a gravel path. Artificial dragonflies, most exaggerated in size, appear profusely among the flora and fauna. A unique group of gnomes have claimed this area and appear in an array of relaxed poses among the varied flowerpots.

Above: **Wild at heart. Gnomes commune with nature.**

Opposite page, left: **Young at heart.**

Opposite page, right: **Domestic bliss: a family of straw-haired gnomes (top right), a leisurely Sunday afternoon (center right) and gnome sanctuary (bottom right).**

Many years ago, Jean decided to name the entire
garden Gnome Man's Land. It was the most fitting
title she could think of to unite all of the separate
gnome gardens. Jim maintains the large, beautiful
green lawn that helps to provide a nice surrounding
common area between the gardens.

Jean has always enjoyed working with gnomes. They
have made her garden a fantasyland. They are easy
to place here and there, and she finds it fun to
arrange groupings that have common interests, bring
out a new theme or elaborate on an old one when
introducing a recently purchased gnome. The
collection now totals well over 800 outdoor garden
gnomes and that number is still growing!

Every collector of gnomes has their own idea of what
sort of collection they want. Some want antique
gnomes and will allow them to continue aging.
However, Jean wants her gnomes to look new with
fresh, bright colors to further embellish the gardens.
Although the gnomes are taken inside during the
winter months, Jean finds that a sizable number have
to be repainted every year. She uses an assembly-line
method, starting with the red or green hats first and
then works down. Usually the flesh color is next,
then the gray beards, green jackets, blue pants and
black or brown boots. Of course, there are always
some exceptions that need special attention.

Their neighbors enjoy the gnome displays too and
like entertaining their out-of-town guests by bringing
them over to the garden for prearranged tours. Over a

Below: **The Frog Concerto.**

Bottom: **Gnomes busily weeding the rockery.**

period of time, eight new gnomes appeared. In time, Jim and Jean realized that friendly neighbors had managed to slip new gnomes in and were waiting to see how long it took before their addition was discovered!

One notable neighborly incident occurred a few years ago, when a newspaper reporter arrived for an appointment one morning to take notes for an article she was writing on gnomes. As Jean led her around the grounds, explaining some of the highlights, she suddenly stopped in the middle of a sentence and blurted out, "Oh my, I've never seen that gnome before!" pointing to the new little stranger. Her husband had told a neighbor the day before that a reporter would be coming over in the morning. The neighbor had purchased a gnome weeks before and had planned to give it to Jim and Jean as a gift. On hearing of the next day's event, she decided to just place it in the middle of the garden early in the morning. The reporter summed it up in her article, "No gnome thievery here—just gifts!"

Jean is often asked if she has a favorite gnome. No, she does not. There are so many, she says, she couldn't possibly single out just one. Every spring she eagerly looks forward to the weather clearing and being able to go outdoors to begin reassembling the gnomes and props in their designated locations. She loves the challenge of adding new ones to exisiting groups, or now and then developing new groupings and scenes.

The gardens are not open to the public but they do have friends, and small groups, such as garden clubs and other organizations, visit from time to time. A typical outing consists of a gnome garden tour, with a break for a picnic with the gnomes. The picnic tables are covered with gnome-print tablecloths and napkins. Plates, glasses and drinking cups have gnome patterns on them, too. Favorite lunch foods are macaroni and potato salads in large ceramic bowls of upside-down red mushroom caps, and sandwiches and assorted fresh fruit are served on gnome-patterned platters. Dessert is always homemade gnome-shaped, decorated cookies, which are always a very big hit with gnomes and people alike!

The gnome garden has earned the reputation as being unique in the U.S. Most people who see the garden have never heard the stories and legends associated with gnomes — such as that they are protectors of the earth, humankind, gardens, homes and treasures. They are absolutely fascinated to learn these things. At the end of a tour, guests are invited to pick a scene that especially appealed to them so that they can be photographed with some of the gnomes.

Over the years, Jean and Jim have received many compliments, some in the form of verbal remarks, others in cards and notes. Gnome collecting has not only brought a world of happiness to them, but their garden has given much pleasure to others.

Left **The culmination of summer—the gnome picnic. Everyone's welcome!**

dutch collections

Forest Gnome

Frits Ruhland lives in a small town north of Amsterdam, but he spends the summer and early autumn months living in Canada in a cottage on his brother's 100-acre (40 ha) forest estate south of Ottawa. Frits's brother is a landscaper and often brings home old garden ornaments, including gnomes, and puts them out in the forest. About 20 years ago, Frits, who has had a fondness for gnomes since childhood, decided to sort out these ornaments. He placed many of them around the cottage and created his first gnome garden. Since then, the

collection has grown. Vintage gnomes are kept inside to protect them from the elements, but there are many gnomes outside, and each year Frits creates a new scene for them, such as a fishing pond, a bandstand, a small gnome village and all kinds of gnome dwellings and gardens. The collection, which now numbers well over 300 gnomes of various sizes, is open to the public for one weekend in September and often attracts more than 200 adults and children.

Right: **A rare vintage French gnome playing the mandolin.**

Above right: **1960s Japanese porcelain gnomes.**

Back in Holland, Frits has a collection in his home of about 250 antique and vintage gnomes of all sizes, together with illustrations, postcards, books, paintings, mugs, tins, key rings, embroidered pictures and old children's toys, all depicting gnomes in some way. He is particularly fond of his old gnomes because of their coloring and facial expressions. Frits makes no attempt to renovate them, believing they deserve to mature gracefully.

Kabouterland

Keeping it in the family, Frits's sister runs Kabouterland (Gnomeland) in Exloo, in the east of the Netherlands. It is a fantasy fairyland for children. At the entrance to the 5-acre (2 ha) site, there is a gnome museum housing about 500 gnomes and there are a further 1,000 gnomes in groups around the site in which there is also a small zoo and a number of other attractions for children.

Below: **Frits Ruhland's "Kinder" miniature gnomes.**

Tiny Little People

Gnomes are popular in the Netherlands and over in Egmond aan zee on the North Sea coast, 59-year-old Theo, a bank employee, has what is probably the largest collection of miniature gnomes in Holland. He began his collection, which has been featured on local television and in newspapers and magazines, about 25 years ago and it now numbers well over 1,000. It all started on a birthday when his sister gave him some brightly colored gnomes for his garden. She continued to give him gnomes over the following years. As his garden began to fill, however, he decided to look for miniature gnomes that he could display inside the house. He very quickly filled one shelf, then another, then another and progressed to a display cabinet.

He was particularly pleased to gather a complete set of the Kinder Surprise series of gnomes to add to the collection, and now he has two display cabinets on the second floor of his home. His gnomes, he says, have a view of the sand dunes—where the real gnomes might be!

Aimed at children, Kinder Surprise is a chocolate egg containing a small toy. Manufactured by Ferrero, it originated in Italy in 1972 and was sold all over the world, although it was subsequently banned in the United States where the toy was deemed a choking hazard. In Europe meanwhile, its popularity spread beyond children and the toys contained inside became a collecting phenomenon. In 1992 there was a series of 10 gnomes. The 1½-inch (4 cm) tall handpainted characters, which became popular with enthusiasts, are modeled in various work activities and are made of hard plastic.

Above left and right: **Theo and his collection of miniature gnomes.**

collections in germany

Gnome Collector—Man and Boy

Thomas Brinkmann lives in a bright and friendly home on the edge of a forest, and visitors are welcomed by a large number of garden gnomes at the front of the house.

When he was a child, Thomas had several gnomes in his parent's garden in Germany. He went on to become a serious collector of gnomes in around 1978 when, on a visit to a market, he came across a gnome that reminded him of his childhood collection. He bought the gnome and today, at his home in Essen, he has more than 1,000 gnomes and a large collection of catalogs, literature, newspaper reports, photographs and postcards relating to gnomes. Working with Frank Ulrich and the Thüringer

Left and below: **Early 20th-century German gnomes.**

Opposite page: **A vintage terra-cotta gnome made by Heissner in Gräfenroda, Germany c. 1890.**

Gnome Museum, he has gone on to establish a reputation as an authority on the history of the garden gnome. He is frequently quoted and has published a number of treatises.

80

Gnome-Park

Frank Ulrich has owned the 54,000-square-foot (5,000 sq m) Zwergen-Park (Gnome-Park) at Trusetal since 1996. The world famous park now displays more than 3,500 gnomes in a variety of arrangements. There is also a shop selling good-quality gnomes and a restaurant for hungry visitors.

The park has a small-gauge railway for visitors to take a journey into a world of gnomes. From the train, they are able to see a lake with gnomes fishing, Snow White and the Seven Dwarfs, a gnome school, a gnome garden and many other displays, all of which are particularly attractive for any gnome photography enthusiasts out there.

In 2004, Frank began a collection of antique gnomes and gnome artifacts, such as catalogs, postcards and maker's molds, all of which are now housed in the Thüringer Garden Gnome Museum, which opened within the park in 2005. The museum has about 1,000 exhibits, including several genuine vintage Maresch, Griebel and Bernhard Bloch gnomes, dating from around 1900.

Gnome-Park is in the heart of southeast Germany, only an hour's drive from Gräfenroda, the birthplace of the garden gnome. In addition to entertaining visitors, the park hosts many meetings, including what must be the world's most important gnome convention, when manufacturers, collectors and gnome lovers gather there to discuss current trends and simply celebrate the garden gnome.

the gnomesville massacre

The breathtaking Ferguson Valley in Western Australia is fast becoming a tourist destination. At the top of a spectacular drive through the rolling countryside is the small town of Wellington Mills, once a busy mill town, now at the center of the Wellington National Park. Within the national park stands the King Jarrah Tree, which at more than 500 years old, is one of the oldest Jarrah trees in the world. But this tree is no longer the main attraction in the area. What was once a very ordinary traffic circle and unassuming stretch of road, is now the focus of much attention.

THERE'S NO PLACE LIKE GNOME-SVILLE

GNOME MAN IS AN ISLAND

Above: **The gnomes tend to these old trees.**

Left: **Gnome literature.**

The traffic circle at Wellington Mills, where Wellington Mill Road joins Ferguson Road, near Bunbury, was built to alleviate a traffic hazard. Nobody knows just exactly how the gnomes started appearing, but rumor has it that it began with one gnome being placed on the side of the road by a local resident to watch over the road building. Within a few months there were about 300 gnomes in residence and within a year there were about 900. It didn't take much longer for the "community" to be estimated at over 1,000!

Left: The gnome well.

Gnomesville, as it came to be known, has gnomes scattered in the bush, alongside the road, and down pathways. Visitors wandering around might think they have seen them all, when suddenly they will find another one peeking down from a tree or from behind a log. This is not just a pile of old gnomes dumped on the side of the road—it really is like a community. Groups of gnomes are playing cricket, flying airplanes and rockets, having parties and much more besides. There is a rock band and many other experiences such as the "Gnoman Empire" and "There's No Place Like Gnome."

Both pages: **A happy community that harbors gnomes who like to garden, DJ, jet off to outer space and even those who believe in a higher power.**

Gnomesville attracts busloads of people every day and has become a popular tourist attraction, promoted by tour companies and printed on tourist maps. People are encouraged to visit and bring their own gnomes, write a message and then leave them to join the community. This has led to a national, and even international, feel to the place. There are gnomes from London, New York, Sydney and many other places from all over Australia and the rest of the world. As one visitor said, "I guarantee that once you have seen this place you will want to leave your own gnome." There are picnic tables for those who want to stay a while and take in the beautiful surrounding countryside.

great gnome
collections

Then tragedy occurred. That scourge of our civilization—vandalism—struck one night in January 2007. A gang of vandals rampaged through Gnomesville, lopping off heads and smashing many of the gnomes. Local newspapers dubbed it "The Gnomesville Massacre" and a reward was offered for the arrest of the villains. Several dozen gnomes are thought to have perished.

Left: **A message to a gnome.**

Above: **After the massacre, the gnomes triage their wounded.**

Opposite page: **The gnomes have built up their community slowly and patiently, and will do so again.**

But gnomes are resilient creatures and, with the help of local residents, they have stoically rebuilt their community. Losses are being replaced, numbers are increasing and a memorial is in place to ensure that those who have gone will not be forgotten.

Gnomesville lives!

87

gnome adventures

gnomes ahoy!

A day trip—Plonker and Lusty Lucy have decided to leave their shady garden and treat themselves to a visit to Branksome Beach in Dorset, England.

Above: Working up the courage to go for a paddle.

Opposite page: Plonker is overwhelmed by the surf.

Above right and right: What a Plonker, showing off again.

gnomes storm chelsea

They said it could not be done, but gnomes did venture deep into the RHS 2007 Chelsea Flower Show in London and made their presence known in the Grand Pavilion. "Mobile Joe" and "Up you Jack" were there to protest against the infamous Royal Horticultural Society ban on the use of gnomes as garden ornaments. The ban has been in place for more than a decade, so the gnomes had no alternative but to express their dissatisfaction with a lighthearted demonstration at the show.

Our two cheeky heroes joined the lineups and introduced themselves to the prizewinners. Everyone was very friendly and they were made extremely welcome. They had their photographs taken in front of the towering Gold Medal–winning lupins and, best of all, in the mystical Carnivorous Plant Society display; Jack headed for the auricula display and was seen posing among the flower pots.

They had a terrific day out and made lots of friends.

There was an "alternative" event! Residents of Chesley Gardens in East Ham, London, with the support of eBay, the online auction site, staged "The Chesley Flower Show 2007" that had royal patronage—two stunning Pearly Queens. Gorgeous gardens were created in a normal East End street and gnomes were made very welcome—they lined up to get in!

Left: **Mobile Joe dwarfed by the spectacular lupins.**

gnomes storm
chelsea

Above: Banned from The Chelsea Flower Show, the gnomes have found a more welcoming show to attend.

Above left: Henry is introduced to a pearly queen.

Left: Despite the Chelsea Flower Show restrictions, Up You Jack and Mobile Joe manage to sneak into a garden—but as intrepid explorers, not ornaments!

93

a swiss comedy

Picture a little white-haired old lady, Joyce, sitting at the front of a coach bus traveling through Switzerland. As they passed through the picturesque villages with their picture-postcard houses and lovely gardens, the driver remarked on how neat the lawns were and how so many were full of gnomes. Joyce quietly replied that the gnomes were there to look after the gardens. "They cut the grass with nail-scissors by moonlight" she said, "and keep things neat and tidy." Out of the side of his mouth, the driver said to the tour manager, "Nutter on board," and he continued to mock gnomes and their owners for the rest of the day.

The next morning, after everyone had boarded the coach as usual, the driver found a note on his dashboard from the "Gnomes R Us" union, warning him that being a "gnomophobe" in Switzerland carried heavy penalties. Throughout the rest of the week, every time he disparaged a gnome, there would be another note—one even appeared on his pillow in his hotel room!

The messages became more outrageous and on one particular day the note warned the driver that the police had been informed of his behavior. By coincidence, that same day, he was waved down by the police routinely checking vehicles. The coach was detained for an hour—apparently the driver did not have all his papers with him—so the passengers found it highly amusing when they saw him sink to his knees and thank the police when he was finally released. When he returned to the bus, he found his dashboard crowded with every kind of gnome the passengers had been able to buy.

For their final evening together, everyone met at a lakeside restaurant. As she entered, Joyce sensed an atmosphere in the restaurant and when she turned to collect a drink, there were two life-size gnomes serving drinks—the driver and the tour manager!

Joyce finally confessed that she was the instigator of the gnome campaign. He laughed and said, "It has been the best week of my working life."

Right: **Miniature gnomes tending the pear blossom.**

gnome adventures

a gnome goes to war

Gnomeland sends gnomes to many countries around the world, so were delighted when an email was received from soldiers of the Light Infantry serving as a force protection company with the British Army in Helmund Province, Afghanistan. They said that as a recreational pastime, they were building a garden in their desert camp and thought that a gnome would be a cheerful feature to add to it. They had discussed which gnome they should have and although there were a number of the lads who would like to have seen one of "The Babes" there, they had finally decided that a traditional gnome for the garden's water feature would be more appropriate. So Fred the Fisherman was ordered.

Fred was drafted by Gnomeland. He was well protected with bubble wrap and polystyrene and placed in a sturdy brown box. He was sent via Royal Air Force Brize Norton in Oxfordshire, England, on his long journey east.

Fred arrived safely in Afghanistan a few days later, but before he could take up his station in the garden, he found himself on active service!

Christmas was then not far away so, as a surprise for the lads, Hot Lips, one of "The Babes" flew out to join Fred.

Opposite page: **Brave Fred takes his turn at guard duty.**

Left: **Hot Lips, just before she left for Afghanistan to cheer up the boys.**

to the south atlantic

We are constantly reminded that gnomes are in all parts of the world and it should not be a surprise that a colony is to be found on the Falkland Islands. There is, in fact, quite a large gnome population on the islands and when Julie and her husband decided to visit their friends there, they were asked to take a gnome to add to their collection, plus 100 fertile duck and chicken eggs. Quite unusual cargo for vacation luggage!

Their trip required a great deal of planning—traveling to the Falklands from the United Kingdom involves a long scheduled airplane journey. The only direct service, in fact, is operated by the Royal Air Force from their Oxfordshire Base at Brize Norton and takes 18 hours flying time with a stop on Ascension Island. An alternative would have been to go via Chile with an overnight stop in Santiago. This trip takes at least 48 hours and with her precious egg cargo, Julie could not afford that kind of delay.

When you arrive in the Falkland Islands, there will always be a friendly smile or a courteous "hello" to welcome you. The pace of life is comforting and it allows you to completely unwind. So when Helmut the gnome arrived with his wheelbarrow, and the duck and chicken eggs, he was made very welcome as he took up residence in his new environment in the tiny settlement of Goose Green.

Everything outside the settlements is known locally as "camp." As you walk the beautiful white sand beaches, wander through the tussock grass or sit on top of a cliff, the wildlife will take the time to come and have a closer look at you, so much so, that you become friends for a while with some of the world's rarest and most precious wildlife. Helmut went off with his wheelbarrow in search of the Gentoo penguins who inhabit the Falkland Islands. From where he stood, among the "diddle dee" (a plant whose berries are used to make jam), he could see that the birds are easily recognized by the wide white stripe extending like a bonnet across the top of their heads. Gentoos breed on many sub-Antarctic islands but their main colonies are on the Falkland Islands and South Georgia. Chicks have gray backs with white fronts. Adult Gentoos reach a height of 30–36 inches (76–91 cm) and are the fastest underwater swimming penguins, reaching speeds of 22 mph (35 km/h).

He then went on to Stanley to admire the famous Whalebone Arch before returning to his new home at Goose Green where one day, perhaps, he will be considered a "kelpe." Helmut agreed that this is a place like no other!

Left: **Helmut and the famous Gentoo penguins.**

Opposite page, top left: **Helmut takes a trip to the Whalebone Arch at Christ Church Cathedral in Stanley.**

Opposite page, bottom: **In a patch of "diddle dee," Helmut poses in front of Stanley Harbor and the wreck of the *Lady Elizabeth*, the only remaining three-mast steel barque in the world.**

Opposite page, top right: **A colony of gnomes make their home in Stanley.**

99

guarding **naturally** over mother earth

Artist and gnomologist Henry Sunderland's main mission in life is to make people smile. While he now devotes most of his time and energy to teaching at the Christchurch Polytechnic Institute of Technology School of Art and Design in New Zealand, he has had a "gnome in his bonnet" since 1975. He has gathered a wealth of information on gnomes, has a collection in his garden at home, and lectures and gives after-dinner talks on the subject.

In 1977, Henry took a gnome named Charlie to the Antarctic and had him placed at the geographic South Pole. The purpose of the trip and taking Charlie was to highlight environmental issues. Charlie was the first gnome to have reached the South Pole. Recent reports from Antarctica suggest that at least five more garden gnomes have followed in Charlie's footsteps and are now residing at the South Pole Station, with 25 to 30 other gnomes on record as living at other bases on the white continent.

Opposite page: **Henry Sunderland with two *c.* 1900 Maresch gnomes.**

Right: **A cold gnome at Halley, the British research base on the Antarctic.**

To further his environmental campaign, Henry decided to take another gnome, this one named Jerome, to the North Pole. However, he found that transportation for the journey was largely dependent on the U.S. Air Force, who apparently were a little concerned about being associated with a gnome named Jerome. Despite the fact that he had even received support from his own prime minister, Henry could only conclude that the U.S. Forces could not see the humor in placing a gnome on the North Pole.

However, gnomes would not leave Henry alone. In 1995 he was the main organizer of the world's first international Gnome Convention. Held in Christchurch, the event was a huge success, with more than 10,000 visitors during the weekend. Almost 300 gnomes and their guardians attended, and one of the main guests was Lampy, the surviving Lamport Hall gnome (see page 42), who flew over specially for the convention. As part of the event, the city of Christchurch was presented with its own gnome, unveiled by the mayor, Vicki Buck, who named him Henry. He now looks over and cares for Christchurch's famous botanic gardens.

Henry Sunderland believes that the garden gnome is increasingly being accepted as a friendly reminder for all of us to take better care of Mother Earth and for this reason he coined the phrase "Guarding Naturally Over Mother Earth" (GNOME). He and his gnomes continue to campaign on environmental issues.

Right: **This photo was taken at 2am on February 4, 1977. Tragically, Charlie's paint was burnt off in a fire in an accommodation hut.**

in too deep

Gnomes can be found all over the world, often in some pretty strange places and unusual circumstances, but did you know that you can find them deep underwater?

Yes, gnomes can be found at the bottom of Lake Wastwater in Cumbria. Wasdale on Cumbria's west coast is a superb corner of Great Britain not normally found by many and yet it is home to some of the most dramatic and diverse scenery in the whole of Cumbria. It is famous for being the home of England's highest mountain, Scafell Pike, and at the Wasdale head, its deepest lake, Wastwater. The lake is 3 miles (5 km) long, 225 feet (70 m) wide and 260 feet (80 m) at its deepest. A diver left a gnome there one day, just for fun. He unwittingly started a trend that certainly caught the imagination of local and visiting divers, as the number of gnomes grew.

Left: **There are no such things as mermaids, only gnomes.**

Local divers said that they had known about the collection for years. "There is a bit of a secret society among divers that outsiders don't seem to know about," said an experienced diver from Carlisle. "But now this secret has been revealed, divers from all over the country have been coming to Wastwater to visit the garden and we have tried to keep it quiet. I have seen about 40 gnomes down there, but there must be more. They are all over Wastwater."

The police regional underwater search unit went in to remove the gnomes after they were blamed for attracting divers to the murky and dangerous depths of the lake, but they have failed to stop divers renewing the collection. Gnomes are now even deeper in the lake, beyond 165 feet (50 m) and out of the reach of the police.

Below left: **Gordon Mackie of Tuscan Divers preparing to take another gnome down.**

Below right: **It was just supposed to be a sail around the bay.**

gnome adventures

Most of the gnomes can be found in Wastwater near an area known as The Pinnacles. One gnome is sitting on a wooden airplane, while another is cemented to a brick. Another has a lawnmower and one has affectionately been called Gordon. Divers made signposts saying "Gnome garden this way." There is even a rope leading directly down to the garden and precise directions to it were published on the Internet.

It is said that the gnome garden was created because there is so little to see in the lake, despite the fact that it has relatively clear water, and it gives divers something to visit. They do say that the gnome garden is a big attraction and people from all over the country have dived to see it, but the amazing scenery of the Lake District must also have an appeal to those who visit the area.

But is Lake Wastwater the only place where gnomes have plunged the watery depths? Now the secret can be revealed. It actually really all began about 15 years ago. Loch Fyne is a sea loch on the west coast of Argyll and Bute, Scotland. It extends 40 miles (64 km) inland from the Sound of Bute, making it the longest of the sea lochs. It is deep, dark, muddy and a bit boring for divers, so Gordon Mackie of Tuscan Divers in

Edinburgh started the whole thing off, as a joke, by making a gnome garden at the bottom of the loch so that divers would have something to look at. Then he put some more gnomes in Scapa Flow, one of Britain's most historic stretches of water. Located within the Orkney Islands, off the northeast coast of Scotland, its sheltered waters have been used by ships since prehistory and it has played an important role in travel, trade and conflict throughout the centuries.

The gnomes in Scapa Flow have been placed at the 20-foot (6 m) decompression stop depth and divers are encouraged to take them to other dive locations just to see where their journey ends.

There are now about 40 gnomes in Loch Fyne and there are many more in Scapa Flow. Other divers began putting gnomes in quarries and lakes and it soon became something of a scuba diver's competition. In addition to Wastwater, there are also gnomes in Loch Long, Layborne Lake near Maidstone and one has even been reported off the coast of Tenerife! Are there any more? They always raise a smile when discovered by divers, but then, they do that on dry land too, don't they?

Right: Loch Fyne is deep, dark and muddy, so scuba divers installed a gnome garden to alleviate the boredom.

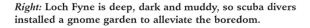

the modbury gnome

The village of Modbury, which dates back to the 11th century, lies in a hollow and is surrounded by the hills and ridges of the South Hams in Devon, England. One summer's day, a builder was walking past a dumpster in the village, when he saw a cute garden gnome struggling to escape from the debris. Feeling sorry for the little fellow, he picked him up, brushed him down and placed him on a wall just outside the village, where he remained for many weeks. The gnome raised a smile from everyone who passed him by and the "Modbury Gnome" became quite famous locally and was adopted by the village.

The mystery of who put the gnome on the wall became a topic of much speculation in the village. Local newspapers, radio stations and patrons of the local pub joined in the friendly guessing game. During the hot and sunny weather that summer, a caller to the local radio station suggested that the gnome would benefit by wearing a pair of sunglasses. When he heard this, the builder, aided by an accomplice, fitted the little fellow with a pair of sunglasses and, of course, this only added to the mystery. Passing bus drivers even began pointing him out to their passengers and his fame started to spread.

Sadly, his fame was his undoing, and one day the Modbury Gnome was stolen. As you can imagine, the builder and the villagers were devastated by what had happened, so our builder went in search of a replacement gnome. He managed to find a fine specimen, but this time he took the precaution of fixing him in position on the wall. Everyone in the village was delighted to see a gnome back in place again.

Tragically, a few weeks later, "some muppet" as the builder referred to the villian, had broken off the top half of the gnome, leaving only the gnome's legs and feet still in place in the cement. The locals were very sad, and even with the help of the local radio station, they could not find out who the culprit was—but then they didn't even know who had put the gnome there in the first place did they?

The real mystery is—who stole the Modbury Gnome?

Opposite page: **All that is left of the Modbury Gnome.**

a very australian convention

The Rotary Club of Lower Blue Mountains has conducted three Australian Gnome Conventions since 2004, at Glenbrook, New South Wales, attracting nationwide and even international attention. Since the first convention, attendance of gnomes has almost doubled, and a small group made the long trip from England in 2006.

Opposite page, far left: **David Cook, the Australian Gnome Convention convenor, 2006.**

Opposite page, left and below right: **Gnomes enjoying themselves at the convention.**

Every gnome in the Blue Mountains area is welcome to attend and invitations are sent to many other countries. In fact, Glenbrook's local gnomes have traveled the world to promote the concept of the convention.

Gnomes traveling long distances are offered overnight accommodation in some of the delightful Rotary gardens, but there have been issues with late-night noise when a group of English gnomes were present. All food and beverage for the gnomes are provided by the Rotary Club.

Gnomes assemble for the convention in a secure area on Glenbrook Park where Rotary's Gnome Convention convenor makes the welcoming speech. Visitors can then observe the gnomes enjoying a variety of activities—fishing, music, gardening and other types of vocational pursuits.

the gnome liberation front

Once upon a time, all was as it should have been in the Stevens's garden. The grass was green, a tableau of Snow White and the Seven Dwarfs was in pride of place on the lawn, spring had sprung and among the daffodils was a workforce of busy gnomes.

But this picture of suburban tranquillity was spoiled early one Saturday morning, when Alice and Jack looked out of the window of their house to find Snow White and her entourage had disappeared. To add insult to injury, the thieves returned the following night, and what had once been a collection of more than 20 gnomes was reduced to four. These little helpers were not "gnomenapped" as they were secured in place with metal stakes.

The police response did not offer much hope for the safe return of the gnomes. "The owners were obviously upset," said the local constable. He had logged the theft as "garden furniture, Snow White plus seven," and said, "Perhaps they will turn up in a car-trunk sale."

However, this is not the only case where owners have had their beloved gnomes taken from them. Garden gnomes have lived a peaceful and pleasant life for almost 150 years. They have harmed no one, given pleasure to many and added fun to gardens all over the world. But stories of gnomes traveling to remote, even exotic locations, and sending postcards home of their travels, are now embedded in

contemporary folklore. Sometimes the owners receive snapshots of the gnome or it is sometimes returned with a shoeshine suntan. Incidents of traveling gnomes became so common that a U.S. travel company launched an advertising campaign based on the idea and their "Roaming Gnome" became something of a traveler's mascot and, some would say, the most famous gnome in North America. Numerous "traveling gnome" websites sprang up detailing the various adventures of gnomes, many showing great imagination and photographic skills.

Modern folklore is often based on a seed of truth. For example, in northeastern France, 11 garden gnomes were found hanging from a bridge in what appeared to be a mass suicide. Police found a note in which the gnomes said they wanted to quit this world and join a sect of the Temple of Submissive Dwarfs. "By the time you read these few words," the note continued, "we will no longer be part of your selfish world which it has been our unhappy task to decorate." Two years earlier, 119 gnomes were discovered in a forest, miles from the town of Aix-en-Provence from which they had mysteriously vanished. Single gatherings of this size are comparatively rare. More often than not, the unfortunate gnomes are rounded up in small groups, sometimes accompanied by a Snow White, and they are repainted blue and green— the colors of the *Front de Libération des Nains de Jardin* (FLNJ) or "The Gnome Liberation Front."

112

Free all gnome

Like most revolutions, the one that mobilized European gnomes in the 1990s might have been fueled by a mix of big business and elitism. There was a climate of stiff competition among German gnome manufacturers who prided themselves on their high-quality product. It is estimated that there are 30 million gnomes in German gardens and inevitably this encouraged a proliferation of cheaper copies from neighboring countries. The German government even banned the import of foreign gnomes, and customs officers began seizing thousands of gnomes being smuggled over the Polish and Czech borders. Foreign-made gnomes then became the target of garden desecration in Germany.

The first reported FLNJ "release" was in the Normandy town of Alençon, when 200 gnomes disappeared. The police later found the haul in a nearby forest. The gnomes were not only repainted, but they were also wearing painted glasses ("to see in the dark" claimed the FLNJ) and adorned with pasta ("so they don't go hungry").

Other "groups" called themselves cells of the The Gnome Liberation Front or operated as independent movements, such as The Red Gnome Army, Free the Gnomes, and *Movimento Autonomo per la Liberazione delle Anime da Giardino* (Independent Movement for the Liberation of Garden Gnomes). These are just a few examples of the groups that began spreading across Europe, many of them setting up websites so that they could link and communicate. Some of these

sites, in a political parody, proclaim a "manifesto" including declarations that "forcing gnomes to stand in gardens without just compensation, against their free will, for the sake of ornamentation, is immoral," and go on to "urge gnomes to rise up and break the bonds of slavery!" In response to this, in Belgium, a self-styled Gnome Protection Squad claimed to have over 300 members to counter these groups. Eventually, public outrage paid off when, in 1997, four men were arrested in Bethune, France, after being caught in possession of gnomes and FLNJ literature. Subsequently, 184 gnomes were recovered from the homes of the arrested men.

In early 2000, several dozen gnomes went missing from an exhibition at the Bagatelle Gardens in Paris. The FLNJ again claimed responsibility, demanding, "This odious exhibition must be closed immediately." The police saw it as a national problem and suspected some form of coordination in reported incidents. Later, 43 gnomes were found in the grounds of the public library in Lingolsheim, Strasbourg. In Rouen, 68 gnomes were recovered from a house after a police surveillance operation.

A website for The Garden Gnome Emancipation Movement appeared to serve as a pool of information on worldwide "gnomenapping" activity, which had spread as far as Australia, Japan and the United Kingdom. These "groups" are, of course, not really groups as such, they are spoof organizations, often initiated by individuals or students and local practical

jokers who have seized on what has become a worldwide phenomenon— "gnomenapping." These "groups" have discovered that gnomes are fun, although their type of "fun" can be very disturbing to many gnome owners.

Alex, a milkman, says his occupation is the perfect disguise for a gnome liberator. He began his undercover role when he "took" two antique gnomes from a garden to decorate his own. Dishonesty turned to irresistible impulse and the excitement of his early morning shift soared. Suddenly, every garden on his milk round blossomed with artistic potential. Often he would simply swap a gnome from one garden to another, enjoying the mischievous feeling of wondering if the owners had noticed that the gnome who was fishing yesterday was now digging. Alternatively, he would provide gnomes for the gnomeless, much to the latter's surprise when they collected their milk from their doorstep in the morning.

None of this is of much interest to Alice Stevens of course. Her husband has now taken to scouring sales hoping to spot their gnomes and perhaps catch the thieves. No luck so far. "It's a shame," says Alice ruefully. "The gnomes gave entertainment and some fantasy for the local kids." For others, somewhere, possibly in your neighborhood, they may still do.

the modern gnome

political satire

Political satire, as a genre, has been with us probably since the time of the ancient Greeks or the forum of ancient Rome. This type of satire is often presented in the form of cartoon drawings, certainly since the 19th century and, more recently, puppets have been used to lampoon politicians on television. Therefore, it is perhaps not surprising that the innocent yet mischievous garden gnome should eventually get in on the act.

In Germany, the birthplace of the garden gnome, politicians and other public figures, such as television personalities, have been caricatured as gnomes since the 1980s to deflate their pretensions. Following in this tradition, in the early 1990s, Jutta and Günter Griebel of Der Zwergenkaufhaus, in Rot am See, Baden-Württemberg, produced a series of ceramic gnomes satirizing the politicians of the day, including (below, from left to right) Theodor Waigel, Helmut Kohl, Jürgen Möllemann and Björn Engholm in "see no evil, hear no evil, think no evil and speak no evil" poses.

Below: **German politicians "see no evil, hear no evil, think no evil and speak no evil."**

During the 2004 American presidential elections, Sam Girton of Georgia began selling a small garden gnome that looked like President George W. Bush. The gnome wore cowboy boots and had his fingers crossed behind his back, and despite, or perhaps because of, its political ambiguity, it proved to be extremely popular during the election season, with members of both parties buying them.

Sam says that his idea for the "Bush Gnome," as it became known, came about because President Bush is often depicted with pointy ears in political cartoons; he thought it made him look like a gnome. His concept was brought to life by Sandy Plunket, who had worked as a comic book artist at Marvel and who sketched it; Erin Payne Bowman, a clay sculptor based in Philadelphia who created the model used to make the molds; and the figures were made by Buckeye Stoneware in Ohio, an area known as "Potteryland, U.S.A." because of its pottery-making history. The figures were handpainted and each one stamped and numbered. The original edition of the Bush gnome, "Dubyah," was limited to a production run of 5,000. It sold out and is now a collectible item.

Left: **The original Bush gnome.**

Other Bush Gnome models are now in production, including:

Lumberjack—Dubyah is wearing a white shirt and is leaning on an axe beside the stump of a tree. This has been interpreted as a reference to the story of the young George Washington cutting down a cherry tree, while others see it as a representation of the destruction of America's natural resources by big businesses.

Traditional—Dubyah is dressed in the traditional gnome "uniform," including the red hat and boots, but he is also sporting his native Texan belt buckle. He is carrying the Stars and Stripes.

Patriotic—this Dubyah is the embodiment of the American Dream.

Military—watch out for this Dubyah—dressed and armed for war, but his combat bootlaces are untied.

Top: **Lumberjack Bush gnome.**

Right: **Patriotic Bush gnome.**

Far right: **Military Bush gnome.**

In the lead up to the United Kingdom's 2005 general election, a set of "political" gnomes was commissioned for a television gardening program in response to what was acknowledged to be an uninspiring election. The gnomes were made as a special project and they represented Tony Blair, the prime minister, digging for weapons of mass destruction; Michael Howard, the then leader of the Conservative Party, in vampire-like mode; and Charles Kennedy, then leader of the Liberal Party, sitting on a fence drinking beer. The gnomes were featured in a number of national newspapers and TV newscasts.

This page: **The 2005 leaders of the Labour, Conservative, and Liberal Democrat parties of the U.K. pose outside the House of Commons. Charles Kennedy (*left*), Tony Blair (*below left*) and Michael Howard (*below right*).**

the naughty gnome

In Germany in 1988, in support of a protest concerning a ban on the display of gnomes in a Hamburg housing estate, Jutta and Günter Griebel created their "Knife in the Back," "Up You Jack" and "Flasher" gnomes. In the 1990s they also began producing a range of rude and naughty gnomes, including "gay" gnomes and the "Tarzan" gnome. All of these were a distinct departure from the appearance of the traditional garden gnome. While many of them were risqué, and some were certainly not suitable for display in the garden, they proved to be a great success among younger people who took them for their humorous rather than decorative value.

ERGE
TYPISCH
DEUTSCH
Folge 2

Das
ZwergenKaufhaus

Left: ZwergenKaufhaus 1990 catalog displaying their new range of gnomes.

Opposite page: Up You Jack, Zwergen Power.

rethinking the garden gnome

The question most often posed is, "Where did garden gnomes come from?" Perhaps the question we should be asking is, "Where are they going?" The German domination of the gnome market has fallen away and changes to the appearance of gnomes continue to evolve. With mass production in Eastern Europe and the Far East, the Disney and cartoon character influence has become more pronounced. The white beard is still there, most of the time, but facially, few of these modern gnomes are little old men. The brightly colored, cherubic gnomes we see in gardens and on the shelves of garden centers today are a far cry from the gnarled, little old men of mythology and the detailed sculpture of early garden gnomes. Traditional garden gnomes can still be found, but they are moving into the 21st century and are as likely to be seen carrying a laptop or mobile phone as they are a fishing rod or spade. These are the new generation of gnomes. Gnome figurines were once popular as household ornaments, then they became garden ornaments, now they are moving indoors again and can be found residing in offices, sporting clubs and banks. Guaranteed to bring out a smile and often a little rude or naughty, they are now given as retirement, birthday and Christmas gifts.

Gnomes are now quirky and fun, but their position in folklore is permanent and they are likely to retain a place in everyone's affections. The continuing worldwide interest in gnomes, for whatever reason, is testament to their popularity.

Above: **Fancy a game of cricket?**

Left: **A modern resin gnome made in China.**

Opposite page, left: **Mobile Joe, a 21st-century gnome.**

Opposite page, right: **Two plastic Heissner gnomes floating in a pond.**

MJ's blog

Hi. The name's Joe—Mobile Joe—or, to my friends, "MJ." I live at Gnomeland—well, some of the time!

Suzanne called me and said, "Come and see me, you'll love London." I said I'd go, but only on the following conditions:

1. I wouldn't be dragged around shoe stores.

2. I could visit a cool mobile phone shop—to see the latest headset accessories—I heard there were a few on Oxford Street.

3. I could get a decent coffee and cake somewhere.

Suzanne (aka "S") picked me up from Waterloo Station and, true to her word, took me to a great place for breakfast, Carluccio's near Selfridges. It's probably one of the best cappuccinos I've ever had.

Quite frankly, I couldn't face walking everywhere (I've got short legs), so S put me in her Topshop bag and we started at the Houses of Parliament (saw Big Ben and its 13-ton bell). The Union Jack was flying on the Victoria Tower, so the Prime Minister was probably in there having his lunch and discussing gnome rights (here, here!).

127

the modern gnome

We visited the Queen for tea at Buckingham Palace but she forgot we were coming (that's me calling her to see where she is). The Guards wouldn't let me through.

Best bit was a ride on the London Eye, great
views over the River Thames and London.
A long day but had a ball—thanks for showing me
around, S. Gotta get back to Gnomeland, 'tho
I could get into this traveling business.

Why not expand my horizons and visit Karen and
James in Chicago and sample the coffee there?

I'm not a big fan of flying and I have put it off for a while. Anyway, I bit the bullet and flew over on a British Airways flight—that's me at Terminal 4 at Heathrow and the British Airways check-in.

Very nice flight—very nice hostesses and they upgraded me to World Traveller Plus! (I had to turn off my phone though—bummer.)

I arrived at O'Hare two hours late and Karen, who was also flying in, was delayed six hours. We missed each other at the airport so I grabbed a taxi to their place. All worked out OK in the end and Karen arrived at the apartment shortly after me.

It was cold and snowing. That's me outside the Wrigley Building on the Magnificent Mile looking forward to my first U.S. coffee.

Blimey, it's soooooooo cold (27°F). Been very busy sightseeing with Karen.

Day started with a search for a local coffee bar.
There's a Starbucks just around the corner from
the apartment, but avoided that as we have loads
of these back home in the U.K. We ended up in a
great place called Pierrot Gourmet—tip top "dry"
cappuccinos and I had my first bagel with cream
cheese. I met Karen's friend Kara—she's lovely.
Flash Harry, I'm not introducing you to her, she
only likes sophisticated fellas—she's mine.

We went up the Hancock Center, wow—great
views of a frozen Lake Michigan and then went
shopping down the Magnificent Mile.

And then guess what? We went to see Rod
Stewart in concert! I was singing "Hot Legs" all
night. Tell you what, the Americans know how to
organize events. No overcrowding or fights to get
out of the parking lot. That's me in the photo
calling Buxum Bess to tell her where I was—she's
a big Rod Stewart fan.

Tired now. Jet lag has got me.

the modern gnome

James got fed up with me whining about the cold so Fed Ex'd me to visit Sharon and Al in Arizona where it's over 80°F. (By the way, although I was packaged well, I still prefer British Airways.)

It's been a great week with the Vandergriffs out here in Southwest U.S.A. They've made sure I had a nice place to sleep and I just loved the pool— after dipping in and out all day they finally wised up and started the pool heater after I turned the same color as my coat. Didn't drink coffee as cocktails seemed in order. Al also educated me on bourbon whiskey. Anyway, I've seen some neat things.

These saguaro (su-war-o) cactuses are amazing— it can take 50 years before they get to be 6 feet tall so the ones in this photo are very old. I've been told that when they get tired at night, they put their arms down but I think Sharon was pulling my leg.

Big Al let me play on the Xbox but he's not much of a sport and kept beating me and wouldn't explain the rules.

I'm heading back to the windy city with Sharon. I'm looking forward to seeing the Grand Canyon from the air. Maybe, on my next visit, I'll get to go to a real rodeo.

135

Kara and her Jeremy invited me to go on an adventure to South America to see the famous Inca ruins called Machu Picchu. They packed me in their backpack and we flew through Miami to Lima, Peru, and then on to Cusco.

'Tho my quest is to have a cappuccino on every continent, I opted for tea in Peru. When we arrived at our hotel, we were brought steaming mugs of coca tea, which is said to help with the acclimatization and to keep the signs of altitude sickness at bay. Pleased to say that the tea worked; it's magic and I only suffered a slight headache. (Mind you I didn't attempt to bring the coca tea leaves home, as that would be asking for trouble!)

We set off in search of Machu Picchu. We were feeling adventurous and decided to hike instead of taking the train. Our trek was 26 miles over four days. I have to say that my little legs had to work double time to keep up with everyone else on the trip! But, as you can see in the picture, I made it safely to Machu Picchu and enjoyed learning about what Inca life might have been like in the town during the early 1500s. Thankfully, the Spanish never found Machu Picchu and therefore did not destroy the structures. When Hiram Bingham discovered the ruins in 1911, approximately 75 percent of the structures were still intact.

As you can see from the pictures I tried calling you fellas at home...no signal!

Did you know that Machu Picchu is vying to be one of the new seven wonders of the world? It is pretty amazing! If you ever have the chance to go—take it! Trust me, if a gnome can make the trek, so can you! Kara, Jeremy...thanks so much for inviting me along, it was a fabulous experience!

Back in Chicago again.

UNITED·STATES

J. Edgar Hoover
FBI
Building

Just back from a tip-top trip to Washington D.C. Karen and James packed me in their suitcase for a short weekend trip to see where the President lives. Flight was on time and, hey, Richard Dreyfus was also on board!

D.C. is a beautiful city and very green (lots of trees and gardens...perfect for a gnome community!). We stayed downtown and on Saturday morning jumped on a bus tour around D.C. Oh my, the memorials were just amazing and HUGE.

We had a hectic weekend—it was 90°F, I got sunburned and my little legs ached at the end of the day, but we packed in loads and had a brilliant time.

1. National Air and Science Museum—saw the Apollo Moon Lander and Gemini and Mercury space capsules (see photo overleaf). Very cool!
2. Jefferson Memorial—it's stunning how Jefferson (the third U.S. President) can be seen through the pillars of the memorial!
3. Vietnam and Korean War Memorials— very moving. I stayed in Karen's bag as I didn't feel comfortable being photographed there.
4. Lincoln Memorial—I loved this (see my pic right!) It's huge and looks out onto the

mj's blog

IN THIS TEMPLE
AS IN THE HEARTS OF THE PEOPLE
FOR WHOM HE SAVED THE UNION
THE MEMORY OF ABRAHAM LINCOLN
IS ENSHRINED FOREVER

Washington monument. The Gettysburg Address is written on the wall. Also, just outside is where Martin Luther King said "I had a dream!"
5. Washington Monument—nearly as tall as the Eiffel Tower—see the pic on page 139!
6. ...and the White House. To be honest the other sights had more impact on me...but it had a nice garden; didn't see any gnomes though.

The highlight for me was the Arlington Cemetery. I just had no idea of the scale and meaning of this place until I saw the Sea of Graves (almost 300,000 service men and their families are buried in the 624 acres of cemetery). I also saw the graves of J.F. Kennedy, the NASA Shuttle Crew and the Tomb of the Unknowns that honors the thousands who have died in battle but have no resting place (by the way, they have now identified the unknown Vietnam soldier through DNA tests).

Saturday evening we went to the Capital Grille for a big juicy steak and a few glasses of vino (yum!) before flying home. On Sunday we went for brunch in Georgetown, which is a great shopping district... It rained all day so I'm glad we did the sightseeing on Saturday!

This should be on every gnome's "city break" list!

On my way back home now. By the way, I looked in on a cool NASA shop!

GOD JUL!

C. LÜCK'S KRÄUTER-THEE

gnome art

One of the most iconic images of 20th-century pop art
must be the cover designed by artist Peter Blake for
The Beatles' album *Sgt. Pepper's Lonely Hearts Club Band*
that was originally released in 1967. Other than
The Beatles, there are 63 people on the album cover,
including Bob Dylan, Fred Astaire, Laurel & Hardy,
Abbott & Costello, Marilyn Monroe, Shirley Temple and
W.C. Fields, but look closely and you will see there is also
a gnome in the picture!

Gnomes have appeared in various art forms over the past 150 years. In the late 19th century they were frequently used on posters, leaflets, books, postcards and advertising material of all types, and it was common to find gnomes advertising anything from laxatives, soap and beer, to cutlery and sewing machines. They were cheerful little characters, offended no one and were very appealing to adults and children alike. Gnomes were an ideal subject to sell a manufacturer's products. In the home, you could find gnomes painted on containers, bottles and porcelain tableware, molded onto ceramic ware, candlesticks and clocks, and featured in jigsaw puzzles and toys.

Above: A 1950s paper doll.

Left: A tin money box made for a U.S. bank in the 1950s.

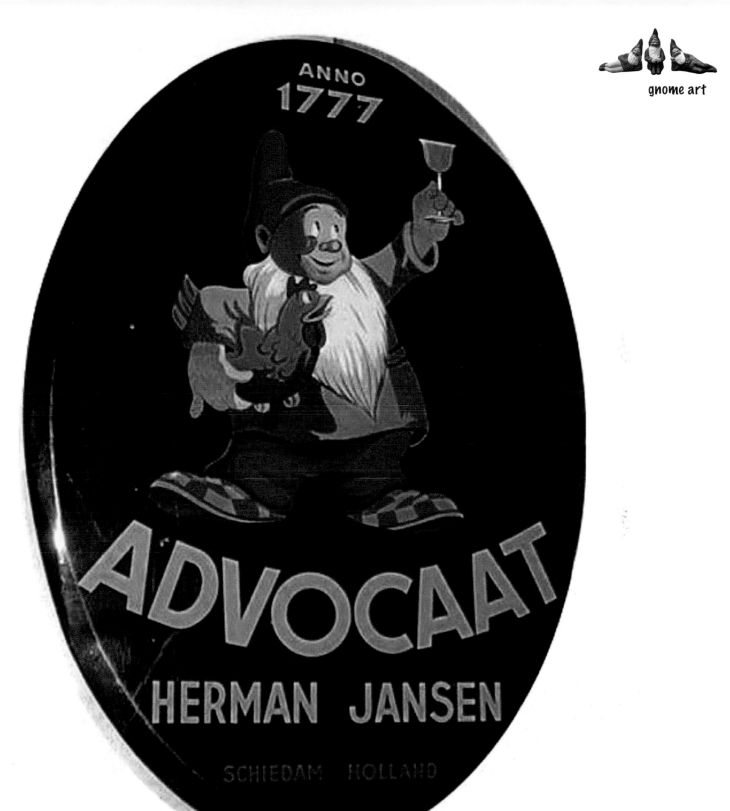

gnome art

Right: A Herman Jansen label.
Part of the Frits Ruhland
collection.

145

In the German city of Cologne, just off the cathedral square, is a fountain known as the *Heinzelmännchen Brunnen*. It is decorated with beautifully carved stone panels that illustrate a story of the friendly heinzelmännchen, or "little workmen" (elves, dwarfs or gnomes), and the tailor's wife. (*Brunnen* means "well.") According to legend, the *heinzelmännchen* assisted the city's craftsmen by doing their work for them while they slept. The *heinzelmännchen*, who are depicted with beards and wearing pointed hats, are said to have left the city after the wife of a tailor, curious to see them at work, scattered peas on the floor of the workshop to make the little men slip and fall. From that time on, the citizens of Cologne have had to do all their work themselves.

Above and right: The *heinzelmännchen* at work. See also page 142, bottom right.

postcards

Postcards were first introduced into North America and Europe in the late 19th century and quickly gained in popularity. By the beginning of the 20th century, the numbers of printed postcards was said to have doubled every six months and the European publishers were exporting millions of high-quality cards. During this period it was still a novelty to receive a Christmas, Easter or New Year's card. Photography was not widely used at the time and most cards were illustrated with drawings and painted in beautiful watercolors. Germany was renowned for having the best printing methods and its cards had the brightest colors and the finest artwork. German domination declined after the First World War when U.S. publishers started producing their own cards. Gnomes had always been a popular subject on both sides of the Atlantic and they continued to be featured on postcards until the 1930s. Gnomes were shown in all sorts of scenes, always happy, cheerful, busy and doing what gnomes do best—making you smile.

There was such a variety of subjects used on postcards that they can be viewed almost as a pictorial record of history. And the fact that gnomes appeared on so many postcards demonstrates, not just in Germany and Scandinavia, but also in the United States, just how much they were enjoyed.

Below: **A New Year's postcard—when the box is open, money cascades out (***right***).**

Das Original befindet sich im Besitz von Kathreiners Malzkaffee-Fabriken.

Die Zwerge sitzen auf der Bank —
Schneewittchen bringt den Frühstückstrank.
Da ruft das kleine Volk: Juchhe,
Jetzt gibt's Kathreiners Malzkaffee!

Above: A 1912 German postcard advertising malt coffee made by the Kathreiner Company, depicting Snow White serving coffee to the seven dwarfs.

Above left: Vintage postcard by Thorvald Rasmussen, *c.* 1905.

Above: An embossed U.S. Easter greeting card *c.* 1910.

Above left: A German advertising card *c.* 1900 for herbalist company C. Lück, promoting their medicines for rheumatism. See also photograph on page 142, bottom left.

Left: An embossed German New Year's postcard *c.* 1910.

149

pottery and ceramics

The Villeroy and Boch factory in Mettlach, Germany, was particularly well known for its beer steins beautifully decorated with gnomes, many of which were painted by Heinrich Schlitt, one of their principal artists.

Gnomes were also an extremely popular subject for the decoration of pottery and ceramic ware, such as beer steins, vases and even dinner services during the 19th and early 20th centuries. The Maresch ceramic factory used the ever-popular gnome to decorate a great deal of tableware and tobacco-related containers, such as thermadors.

Above: **A painted bowl by Dutch artist, Maria Huyben.**

Right: **Heinrich Schlitt's stein, "The dwarf in a nest" was made by V & B Mettlach. Schlitt was well known for his whimsical and sometimes comic gnome paintings.**

When Royal Doulton in England produced their "series ware," designer Charles Noke probably thought of the sets, consisting of plates, bowls and jugs etc., as being collectible. The series was decorated with a number of subjects, including nursery rhymes, scenes from Charles Dickens novels, and there were two with scenes featuring gnomes. "Gnomes A," *c.* 1910, showed a gnome bowing to a fairy, two gnomes smoking on toadstools and a gnome talking to a rabbit, on plates and jugs. "Gnomes B," which was in production up to about 1950, had scenes depicting a number of gnomes among tree roots on plates, cups, saucers, bowls and jugs. The gnome series became known as "Munchkins" in the United States.

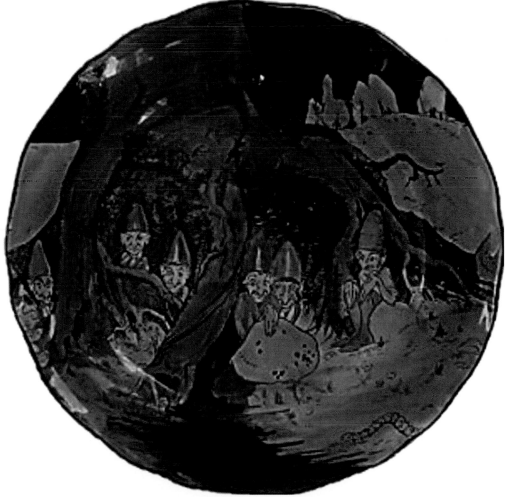

Above: **A stoneware ceramic tankard, *c.* 1900.**

Right: **A bowl from the Royal Doulton "Gnomes B" series. See also the plate on page 142, top right.**

cartoons, illustrations and paintings

The Brothers Grimm story of *Little Snow White* is a very well-known fairy tale and has been illustrated in many ways in its published form by several artists. When Walt Disney brought out his famous *Snow White and the Seven Dwarfs* animated film in 1937, after three years of work by a team of animators, his version of the dwarfs gave each of them an appearance matching the cute characters he had created. They gained worldwide popularity and began to influence the shape of the modern garden gnome, except perhaps in Germany and Scandinavia where the traditional form prevailed.

Jenny Nyström (1854–1946, see also page 10) was best known for her Christmas artwork, which is still popular in Sweden and the other Scandinavian countries. A prolific artist, she painted illustrations for books, magazines, posters and advertisements as well as landscapes and portraits, but she was most famous for her *tomte* postcards and Christmas cards.

Nyström's son, Curt Nyström Stoopendahl, was also a successful popular postcard and poster artist; her brother-in-law, Georg Stoopendahl, too, was an artist

152

Above: **A 1950s fairy tale mural by Herbert Rasch of little Snow White and the seven dwarfs for a German classroom.**

Left: **Extract from C.F. Ortlepp's chromolithograph catalog, *c.* 1900–1920, Germany, showing hand-painted tin garden figurines.**

Left: **Lothar Meggendorfer often used gnomes to illustrate his pop-up books.**

Below: **Ann Fawssett Atkin watercolor,** *The Pond At Night.*

Ann Fawssett Atkin, RASA, is a prolific painter of wildlife and landscapes in England. She has maintained a lifelong love of nature, especially birds, wild flowers and butterflies, that she has painted since early childhood. Unsurprisingly as the founder of The Gnome Reserve (see pages 54–59), her work now often includes fairies and gnomes.

who had a more commercial sideline in Christmas cards and postcards. *Tomten* appeared in both their work, inspired of course, by Jenny Nyström's.

Rien Poortvliet (see also page 16) was already recognized as a book illustrator and for his drawings of animals and scenes of nature before he teamed up with Wil Huygen to illustrate their famous *Gnomes* book. He created what has become known as the "Poortvliet gnome," with his tall conical hat, which went on to captivate people all over the world.

Another illustrator who often used gnomes as a subject was Lothar Meggendorfer (1847–1925), a German artist who was particularly well-known for his pop-up and movable books, many of which had complex mechanisms and multiple levers. He illustrated about 200 such books and they are now highly valued and collected.

the gnome lady

Once upon a time, long ago, in a house high in the hills above Bradford in West Yorkshire, England, there was a little girl whose favorite pastime was making and painting plaster casts of Walt Disney's *Snow White and the Seven Dwarfs*. She used to display them around her bedroom or give them as gifts to her friends.

That little girl was me.

I could not have imagined that one day I would be sharing gnomes with the world.

A little late in life I must confess, I had obtained a computer. As a complete novice, I enrolled at my local training college for a six-week basic Internet course, part of which involved building a one-page website. We all had to choose a subject and mine was garden gnomes. Everyone asked, "Why?" Well, I thought a light-hearted subject would be appropriate and I had inherited some garden gnomes from the previous owner of my house. I had thought them amusing and, having just bought myself a digital camera, I found they photographed well and I decided they made an ideal subject for my web page. Other students also found the subject of gnomes amusing and we all shared jokes about my website. Then one day, one of my fellow students sent me a photograph of a gnome in his garden. Soon I had others being sent to me—some anonymously! But the website made us all laugh. Gnomes were fun.

Gnomeland had been created. After completing the course, I became more and more intrigued with the little chaps, so I looked into the history of gnomes and went on to develop the website further. At first it contained just historical and contemporary information about garden gnomes, together with news items and then, for entertainment, I created some jigsaw puzzles and animations. The big day arrived when I published my site on the World Wide Web—www.gnomeland.co.uk had arrived!

First of all—it worked! And then, to my surprise and enormous pleasure, I found myself coming into contact with a large and very widely spread "gnome fraternity." These were friendly people, nice people, who liked gnomes, collected gnomes and enjoyed gnomes. Several of them became regular correspondents and contributors to the website with their often humorous stories about gnomes. A few dozen hits grew to hundreds, then the website began to attract thousands of hits from around the world. My inbox was regularly overflowing as many of my new friends sent me photographs of their gnomes.

Together with images I had already gathered, to my amazement the site grew to contain the World Wide Web's largest collection of gnome pictures. Even images of gnomes, such as those in postcards, book illustrations and ceramic decoration, were as interesting as the gnomes themselves and I began to gather them into the website.

the gnome lady

Having lived a busy life in many parts of England, bringing up and supporting a family, I was now settled in a picturesque cottage in the New Forest National Park that boasts some of southern England's most beautiful countryside. I found that here I could indulge my passion for gardening and also give time to my new little friends and share them with the world.

That little girl from Bradford might have matured in years, but gnomes were once again giving me a great deal of pleasure.

Gnomes may have been banned from the Chelsea Flower Show in London by officials of the Royal Horticultural Society, but the mere mention of gnomes is enough to make most people smile. I have found that there is, in fact, a resurgence of interest in gnomes, both traditional and new. As they have evolved and adapted to the modern world, they have found new enthusiasts and have reached what some have described as an almost iconic status.

It became obvious to me that there is a lot more to garden gnomes than the rather tacky and cheap, spray-painted, plastic versions of what had once been a very popular garden ornament. In addition to the brightly colored characters we see displayed in many gardens today, there are still the genuine, vintage, traditional gnomes that are much sought-after. There are also postcards, greetings cards, pictures and book illustrations featuring traditional gnomes, together with original illustrated catalogs from gnome manufacturers, all attracting a growing interest from collectors worldwide.

To add further interest for me, I found that the pedigree of old gnomes can often be difficult to establish. I had accumulated a great deal of information since I began championing gnomes and this now enables me to help enthusiasts and collectors in identifying gnomes and their makers.

Following the initial publication of the website, I began receiving many requests for information about where good-quality ceramic gnomes could be bought. Adding a shop to the website seemed to be the next logical step, but this really was a challenge to my computer "skills." That I managed it, without help, was something that gave me great satisfaction. I chose to specialize in ceramic gnomes, which were previously virtually unobtainable in the U.K. The manufacture of ceramic gnomes is a shrinking industry. Even in Germany, the birthplace of the garden gnome, there are very few companies still producing good-quality ceramic gnomes. After a great deal of research—with my English–German dictionary at my side—I obtained stock from Germany and opened the shop on the Internet just before Christmas 2005. The first gnome was sold within days to an enthusiast in Florida! The next delivery was to Montana. I was in the export business! Now I am sending them around the world—from the Isle of Skye to the Falkland Islands. My friends at the post office were soon calling me "The Gnome Lady"!

index

index

acknowledgments

My thanks and enormous gratitude go to my dear friend George, who was always there when I was lost for words, and without whose support and help I could never have completed this project.

A very special thank you goes to my lovely daughters Karen and Suzanne and their friends Kara and Jeremy Schupp and Sharon and Al Vandergriff who took Mobile Joe on his travels.

For sharing their stories with me, I thank:
Gordon Mackie and Tuscan Divers for In Too Deep
Ann Atkin and the Devon Gnome Reserve—A Magical Place
(www.gnomereserve.co.uk)
The Lamport Hall Preservation Trust for their history (www.lamporthall.co.uk)
The RHS Lindley Library for excerpts from *The Garden*
Allison Devine and her Garden for George (www.garden-for-george.com)
Bob Aitken and the Australian Gnome Convention
Brian Kibler for his and the Maresch history
(http://home.earthlink.net/~artifactsco/maresch/)
Cumbrian Newspapers for the quote from their Wastwater article
Philip and Christine Havard of Havard & Havard (www.havardandhavard.com)
David Cook and the Australian Gnome Convention
Frank Ulrich and Zwergen Park (www.zwergen-park.de)
Frits Ruhland and his Dutch collection
Graeme Olson for the Gnomesville Massacre
Henry Sunderland for Guarding Naturally Over Mother Earth
Jean Fensterman and Gnome Man's Land
Jenny for the Modbury Gnome
Joyce Oliver and A Swiss Comedy
Julie Young and her journey to the Falkland Islands
Jutta and Gunter Griebel for their gnome history
Liz Spera and Gnome Habitat U.S.A.
Palle and Kirsten Petersen for a Danish perspective
Rienhard and Iris Griebel for their history and for still making gnomes
(www.zwergen-griebel.de)
Rob Irving for the Gnome Liberation Front
Royal Doulton Archives
Sam Girton and his Bush Gnomes (www.bushgnome.com)
Theo van Gend for his Dutch Collection
Thomas Brinkman for his gnome research.
Taylor Herring Ltd (www.taylorherring.com)
Also, a special mention for my publisher Kyle Cathie, for having faith in me. Muna Reyal, Editorial Director, with Clare Hubbard, copy editor, Sha Huxtable and Alice Holloway, production, and Geoff Hayes, who did the stunning design work, have been a delight to work with and I cannot thank them enough.

Finally, we must all be grateful to the gnomes. Without them there would not have been a book.

The author and publishers would like to thank all the following for kindly giving permission to reproduce their photographs in this book:

Front jacket: Volker Schumann
Pages 2, 40 bottom, 66, 67, 68, 69, 70, 71, 72, 73 and 74: Jean Fenstermaker
Page 5: Mike Scott
Pages 10 bottom left, 142 top left: Jenny Nyström/Kalmar Läms Museum/DACS 2007
Pages 12 bottom left, 13 top right, 14, 80, 81: Thomas Brinkman
Pages 20 right, 31 left: Devon Gnome Reserve
Page 153 bottom right: Ann Fawssett Atkin
Pages 9 right, 22, 23, 26: Rienhard Griebel
Pages 32, 33, 38, 45, 46: Brian Kibler
Page 36: Jennifer Sterchele
Page 37 top right: Candice Kimmel
Page 42: RHS Lindley Library
Page 43: Lamport Hall Trust
Page 44: Barry Feinstein
Page 47: Philip and Christine Havard
Pages 49, 50, 51, 52, 53: Allison Devine
Pages 60, 61, 62, 63, 64, 65: Liz Spera
Pages 76, 77, 144, 145, 150: Frits Ruhland
Pages 78, 79: Theo van Gend
Pages 82, 83, 84, 85, 86, 87, 88 right, 159: Graeme Olsen
Pages 88 bottom left, 100, 101, 103: Henry Sunderland
Page 93 top left and right: eBay Chesley Gardens
Page 96: A soldier
Pages 98, 99 top left and bottom: Julie Young
Page 99 top right: Claus Qvist Jessen
Pages 104, 105, 106, 107: Gordon Mackie
Pages 110, 111: Bob Aitken
Pages 116 left, 121: Taylor Herring Ltd
Pages 24, 25, 34, 118, 122: Gunter Griebel
Pages 119, 120: Sam Girton
Pages 116 bottom right, 132, 133, 138, 139, 140, 141: Karen Egleton
Pages 134, 135: Sharon and Al Vandergriff
Page 139: Kara and Jeremy Schupp

We have made every effort to contact the owners of photographs used in this book but if we have inadvertently omitted to credit anyone, please contact the publisher and we will include in future editions.